Going to the Motherland

things to know for your journey

Sarah Blight

Going to the MotherLand
things to know for your journey

All rights reserved
Copyright © 2011 by Sarah Blight

No part of this book may be reproduced or transmitted in any form or by any means, electronic or mechanical, including photocopying, recording, or by any information storage and retrieval system, without permission in writing from the author.

This book is not intended as medical advice. Its intention is solely entertainment, educational, and informational. Please consult a qualified medical or health professional if you have questions or are in need of medical assistance.

Neither the author nor contributors are engaged in rendering medical advice or services to the individual reader. The ideas, procedures, and suggestions contained in this book are not intended as a substitute for consulting a qualified physician and obtaining medical supervision regarding any activity, procedure, or suggestion that might affect your health. Neither the author, contributors, nor the publishing company shall be liable or responsible for any loss, injury, or damage allegedly arising from any information or suggestion in this book. Please do not sue us. We have no money.

ISBN 978-0-9843347-2-8
ISBN 0-9843347-2-6

PRINTED IN THE UNITED STATES OF AMERICA

acknowledgements

Okay, so I've never done this before. Isn't this the part of the book that's kind of like an Oscar acceptance speech, except, not really? Sweet. Here goes.

First of all, I would like to thank ~~the academy~~ all of the, sometimes, random people who helped me on my journey to the MotherLand and therefore contributed to my debut book- the guy at the gelato stand who told me that my kid was going to be a boy, the anonymous co-workers who commented daily on my ever expanding waistline, the lady at the post office who held the door open for me as I waddled towards her, package laden and panting and then exclaimed "you poor thing, pregnant in this heat", I can't forget my hormones who did not disappoint, they provided much fodder for this book. I must not forget "my first"- the doctor I broke up with, and my subsequent dream team of midwives and doctors whose empathy, warmth, care and compassion were exactly what I needed to give birth with confidence.

I would also like to extend a hearty thank you to my mama who birthed me from her hippie loins and encouraged my writing from a young age, in the form of countless book reports and creative writing assignments she gave me as my teacher.

[Music is cueing]

This is where I talk super-fast and blurt out that -I am blessed with an incredible family of cheerleaders and encouragers who have told me countless times that I'm the next Irma Bombeck. While I'm still too young to really know what that means, I'll take it as a compliment.

To mama & Steveo who read and re-read and helped me refine this book over and over, thank you! A huge thank you (and I can never repay you but I'll try) to the incredible mamas- Chotchers, Laur, Meli, Amy, and Jenny who poured over this book and gave very helpful insight on how to make it better!

A huge thanks to the mamas who let me pick your brains about your birth experience and use them as illustrations in my book.

I received such encouragement and help from Kelli Stapleton and Freedom of the Press Publishing. Thank you so much for your excitement, your gentle prodding, your help and for now (apparently) stalking me.

I am honored to be surrounded by such strong and amazing friends and mothers who have shown me the ropes while allowing me to find my own way, when needed. Love you all!

For You.

table of contents

preface		1
one	Chargin' Towards Pregnancy	13
two	I'm Pregs, Now What?	29
three	Super Dad	69
four	Tough as Nails	81
five	The Gift of the Pelvis	109
six	Decisions, Decisions	125
seven	Is It Go Time?	139
eight	Keep the Party Going	147
nine	Stick a Fork in Me, I'm DONE!	157
ten	The C-Section Scene	177
eleven	After Shocks, What the Hell Just Happened?	191
twelve	Breast Friends Forever	209
thirteen	Getting Your Groove Back	221
fourteen	Putting It All Together	233
contact		237
glossary of terms		241
sources		245

preface

My due date was August 24th, so I was quite surprised when at 2:30am on Wednesday, August 5th, I woke up suddenly and felt compelled to go to the bathroom and realized that a Niagara Falls type event was underway—when I say under I mean there. I barely made it to the bathroom, gave a quick, urgent shout to my husband and we were both shocked that this was happening. There was no doubt in my mind that this was, in fact, my waters breaking. We called the doc and she told us to go back to bed and get some sleep.

Of course, there was no way I could sleep after that. I mean seriously, I was about to have my first baby. It's not like it was my first time getting a perm or something. My head was spinning, I was "ready" in terms of all our baby stuff and mentally I was set for our bambino to arrive, but I had a laundry list of work items, laundry, household stuff, and errands to run. My mind was going 200 miles an hour. Sleep eluded me. My husband was sound asleep in 2 seconds; how he does that, I still don't know. I finally gave up around 5:30 and started some last minute "turbo nesting" which consisted of emailing, organizing, packing, and cleaning. I felt really calm and peaceful and really excited.

One of my desires for this birth was that my mom would be able to make it from Cincinnati (we were in Austin). I wasn't sure how this would be able to happen, but I really wanted it so much. As Niagara Falls was happening, the second phone call I made was to my mom. I had to tell her as early as possible to drop everything and hop on a plane 'because a baby was coming in the next day or so.'

My mom was on high baby alert at this point and a phone call at 3:00 in the morning only meant one thing: baby time. My mom told me later that she was so amped up and freaked out about baby coming that she was running around the house in the middle of the night saying, oh crap oh crap oh crap. She called the airlines to book her flight and started crying, telling the poor ticketing agent that her grandbaby was about to be born and he was three weeks early and her daughter lived in hotter than hell Texas, and that her daughter's water broke (and a million other details that were a little "TMI," especially over the phone at 3am). As soon as mom was finished giving the ticketing agent super-duper important details, she ran up and down the stairs and up and down some more, having no clue what to pack and what she was even doing. This is one of the many reasons I love my mom: her spazzoid tendencies when she's excited about something.

Back to "Hotter than Hell" Babyland: We went to the doctor's office, where a midwife confirmed that indeed my water was broken and I was in early labor. We decided to celebrate and go to Magnolia's, a fabulous Austin breakfast spot, and then head home for a nap. I have to say that sitting there waiting for my pancakes and eggs to arrive as Niagara Falls was still going on was mildly disconcerting. It was strange to know that people around us were blissfully unaware that I was in labor and that we were about to have our lives changed forever.

After breakfast I called my doula, who it turns out, was out of town for a doula conference! I was so bummed that she was going to miss this birth, but overall felt joyful and peaceful. Our original doula actually connected us with her back up, Amanda, who I called and touched base with. She assured me that she was packed and ready to help us if/when we were ready. I took a Tylenol PM and hit the sack. Of course, I had restless sleep, and after 3 hours, I gave up and found that my mom had arrived! I called the doula again and told her that I was having some contractions, but they were very sporadic. She encouraged us to go to the mall and start walking. So that's what we did for about an hour. We, along with the senior citizens of Austin, walked with purpose around the mall. My contractions first felt just like period cramps, but then they started intensifying. It's really hard to describe how they feel. The closest thing I can think of is a super intense tightening around the entire midsection of my body down to my pelvis, but with a deep, inward tightening. The contractions started getting longer at this point, but still nothing substantial.

We headed back home and ate dinner, and I continued staying active, climbing stairs, squatting and doing laundry. We called the doctor, who told us to take our time coming in to the hospital and said she would meet us there later on. So we finally headed in, but not before stopping to buy a video camera on our way. Of course, in the flurry of activity, we didn't even take many videos, but that's another story for another time.

At this point in the story, I was still feeling super calm. I was wondering what true contractions felt like and was hoping that I would be able to progress without the help of drugs. I think I was still in disbelief that this was happening, since I told myself that especially with our first child, I would probably not give birth until 42+ weeks.

Our doula was waiting for us when we arrived at the Women's Center. We got checked into our room and started getting to know our new doula. The plan was to meet her, send her home and call her back when contractions were cranking. But no sooner had we stepped foot inside the hospital door, than the contractions started intensifying and getting a bit closer together. By about 9:30pm, my contractions were lasting about 45 seconds and were about 5 minutes apart. Amanda decided that she should probably stay. I started working through the contractions using the birthing ball in different positions. The most important thing for me was to focus. I didn't want any noise or distractions. I just focused on my breath the entire time. Amanda started suggesting various helpful things to my mom and Steve…like stroking my back, or giving me counter pressure, etcetera. Dr. C came in around 10:00pm and my contractions were now 3 minutes apart and lasting a full minute. Our original plan of her giving me some sleeping meds and then possibly starting Pitocin in the morning was now set aside. I was ecstatic. I really wanted to do a natural labor from start to finish, but had decided earlier in the day that if I had to have Pitocin to speed up my contractions, then I'd just need to go with the flow. I reminded myself that my ultimate goal was to have a healthy baby, but much to our delight, things were progressing on their own. Thank you, God!

It's no secret that I'm a pretty verbal person. Going through labor was no exception. There may have been some (or lots) of moaning involved. I pictured each contraction like a wave and told myself that with each one, I was one closer to the baby, the ultimate reward! Amanda suggested I switch positions to keep from hitting a stalemate with the contractions. As I got out of the bed, I started feeling panic and fear. I felt so much pressure in my pelvis that I almost psyched myself out. Amanda gently reminded me that this was normal and not to be scared. The reassurance was just what I needed. So I decided to hit the shower and got in there with the birthing ball. Steve had the shower head in his hand and ran warm water all over my back. I do recall sternly telling him NOT to get the back of my hair wet. A girl has to have good hair for the birthing pics!

As soon as I sat on the ball, all the pelvic pressure was relieved and I was in heaven. It felt so great! The contractions really started intensifying and getting closer when I was in the shower. I stayed there for almost an hour. Then I suddenly had enough, it didn't feel good anymore. So I stood up, once again feeling slightly panicky at how much pressure there was in my pelvis. I went back to bed, lying on my side. By now things were really picking up. I had a minute between contractions and they were very strong. I started moaning pretty loudly and shaking. I also felt the urge to vomit, which made me feel kind of scared because it felt like I had no control over the shaking in my body and the vomiting. Amanda once again reassured me that this was normal and that my body was preparing me to deliver my beautiful baby by making room. Earlier, Amanda had put some lavender oil on my pillow. The second I stuck my nose in there, I was in heaven. It was so soothing and made me feel like I was at a spa (which lasted approximately 30 seconds). When I started vomiting, she had peppermint oil on hand that she lightly passed over my nose, to help with the nausea. My eyes were closed the entire labor, I was in a zone. But hearing Amanda's, my mom's and Steve's voices reassured me that I was getting closer to having the baby and that what I was feeling was "normal."

Around this time, I felt desperate to be done with labor; I remember thinking, now I know why people use drugs during birth. I really wanted drugs, but I was resolved to see this through. I was so close. I hit transition and my whole body was shaking uncontrollably. The nurse checked me and I was 9 cm dilated. There was just a portion of my cervix that wasn't completely flat. I was really wanting to push at this point...they told me to hold off because if my cervix swelled, I would make it worse for myself and have to wait longer. I started feeling frustrated that I wasn't a 10 yet. Earlier in the evening, the nurse had said that the baby was really low and that it probably wouldn't take very many pushes for me to get the baby out. I think this sort set me up for disappointment, because in my mind, that meant 3 pushes and he would be out. Finally, the doctor came in and told me I could do some half pushes to help warm up my perineum, to avoid unnecessary tearing. Finally, I was given the green light to fully push. I was on my back in the bed, holding my knees. I did NOT expect to give birth in this position, I was hell bent on squatting or being on my hands and knees. But once again, my body dictated my position. This was the one that was the most comfortable for me. After several pushes, I was really frustrated. I wasn't pushing effectively. Who knew pushing could be so hard? The doctor told me to zone in on her fingers and to push her fingers. She also told me to quit grunting and contorting my face, that I was wasting precious energy. I tried a few more pushes with a little more success, but still not as successful as I WANTED. I had to accept that I wasn't finished yet with this job to get the baby out. The doctor said, "Okay, I know you do yoga, let's try a yoga pose." I remained on my back, I put the soles of my feet together and brought them as close to me as I could (fortunately, I am really flexible in this particular pose), I held my feet with my hands, drawing my feet towards me and letting my knees completely relax. I then bore down and really focused all my energy on pushing the doctor's fingers, trying hard not to grunt or make faces. Now things really got moving and the baby moved down the canal.

The doctor asked if Steve wanted to help deliver and he eagerly jumped right in. In between contractions, she was telling him how and what they were going to do. We still didn't know the gender of the baby, so he said he wanted to be the one to tell everyone.

This was about the time that the doctor mentioned to me that the baby was about to crown and I would feel "the ring of fire." I remembered that from our birthing classes and the next few pushes about sent me! I remember thinking; Johnny Cash has no idea what the hell the ring of fire is all about. I silently swore in my head. This was off the charts painful. But I knew that I was so, so, so close to meeting our bundle of joy. I could hear Steve say, "Honey, you are so close, I can see our baby's head, it's coming!" Hearing his excitement gave me the resolve to give the next few pushes my all. Three pushes later and the baby was out. I did open my eyes when Steve said, "Here's the baby's head." The next thing I saw was the head coming out, followed by a white body. I felt a rush of relief, emotionally and physically. I was the first one to see that the baby was a boy. My legs started trembling and Steve put the baby on my chest. I was crying and said, "Jackson William, you're here." He was born at 2:56am, 6 pounds 4 ounces and 20 inches long.

My journey to the MotherLand was only just beginning.

one
Chargin' Towards Pregnancy

You should never say anything to a woman that even remotely suggests that you think she's pregnant unless you can see an actual baby emerging from her at that moment.
~Dave Barry

It was spring of 2006; I had had enough of the manmade hormones coursing through my veins, thanks to the oral contraceptive that I had been taking for years. I decided that I wanted to go back to nature and do this naturally—by do this, I'm referring to family planning. At the time, our family plan was to not have a family…yet. Oh yes, we could definitely picture ourselves the happy family of 8, yes 8, traveling the country, going on adventures and taking time to smell the roses along the way (because isn't that what the reality of 6 kids would be?). The year 2006 was not the year for us to start living out our VonTrapp family dream, we just knew as wonderful as family would be, we weren't ready for it quite yet.

After talking to some of my best girlfriends about the topic, I took the plunge and started taking charge; taking charge of my fertility that is. This was a great decision for me because I'm a "take charge" kind of person. The book, Taking Charge of Your Fertility by Toni Weschler, was a fabulous guide for an anatomically challenged person such as myself. I had no idea where my bits and pieces were located and for sure had zero clue about the job description and responsibilities of them, except for the obvious. Taking Charge of Your Fertility teaches the Fertility Awareness Method (FAM), which basically means you become attuned to your body's menstrual cycle, beginning with charting your temperature each and every morning so that you know when you're ovulating and therefore when to pull the trigger, if pregnancy is your aim, or to when to put the gun in the holster, if you're not ready for kiddos yet. Suffice it to say, thermometers became a mainstay on my bedside table. I say thermometers, plural, because one of the most important things about taking your temp is to not get up or make any big movements, because those movements will inevitably change your temp. So imagine, every morning my alarm goes off and out from under the covers a hand shoots up and rummages around the top of the bedside table, looking for the nearest thermom. Upon victorious attainment, the hand disappears once again under the covers to ascertain my daily temp, whereupon it is written on a chart, so I can start seeing my patterns and getting to know my cycle. And thus, get to know myself.

I will say that getting to know your cycle really feels good. It feels like you're in touch with yourself. (No, I did NOT say "touching yourself." Get your mind out of the gutter!) It's amazing how our bodies really do tell us what's going on, if we just stop and pay attention. So that's my first piece of advice for those of you trying to get pregnant (or trying to avoid it): Get to know your body. And not necessarily in the Fried Green Tomatoes—let's bust out a mirror and discover our female bits—kind of a way. I'm talking about Taking

Charge, knowing your cycle and when you're the most fertile and when you're not.

How to See If You're Fertile Myrtle

1. **Establish your "normal."** What's your normal temperature? What's your normal cycle length? Start noticing these things by charting your temperature each and every morning. Give yourself a few months to notice your patterns. You can chart it on graph paper or using the charts at the back of the Taking Charge of Your Fertility book or download a template online; either way, write it down so you can start noticing patterns.

2. **Pay attention to your bodily fluids.** Did you know that your womanly parts excrete—just winced, sorry. I really don't like that word. It totally sounds like what it is. Ew.

Did you know that your womanly parts manufacture and produce (much better) cervical fluid? I'm sure you did, since you probably buy loads of panty liners each and every month. What you may not know is that the type and consistency of this fluid changes. I need to point out that men always produce fluid, it's called seminal fluid- men are always fertile. After your period, you will probably be pretty dry in the vaginal (vadge) department. Then you'll notice that things start getting sticky and kind of dry and crumbly. The next type of fluid you'll make is creamy in texture and milky white or a bit yellow. Things can get a bit watery and then comes the slippery stuff. It's super stretchy and usually clear, streaked or opaque; this is when you're FERTILE MYRTLE!!The reason it's this consistency is so that it can facilitate the union of the egg and spermies. Isn't that fascinating? Then you dry up again and then it's time for Aunt Flow to come.

I just want to make sure you know that this explanation in no way replaces reading Taking Charge of Your Fertility. This is meant to be a primer. Definitely get your booty online or go to your favorite book store right now and get the book. It's a very thorough and wonderfully informative book, no matter what your family plan is.

3. **The guys' favorite part: practice.** Once you've determined that you're ovulating, it's go time! Practice, practice, practice. (okay, not really, but if there are any guys reading, this is for you). In reality, it only takes one time to get pregnant, so you don't need to procreate like rabbits to get the job done, unless, of course, you want to.

Did it Work?

It took seven years of marriage, thousands of reminders from people- who will remain nameless (cough-grandma,mom,grandma-cough) that I am no spring chicken, my clock is ticking and to get on this baby making train already for the love of the Lord- finally though, all familial heckling aside, we were ready to expand our family.

I have to admit, after all the reading I had done, the charting, the cervical fluid noticing, the in-tuneness with my body, I still had doubts. I constantly doubted whether or not I could get pregnant. It wasn't necessarily a self-doubt of "will my body be able to get pregnant?" It was more along the lines of "without reading the book every step along the way, will I remember everything I need to in order to get this party started?" I kind of felt like I was the cruise director on board a big-ass ocean liner, except I had only read a book (a very good book, mind you) about the job. My husband was blissfully unaware of the pressure of my newly self-proclaimed job title. He was excited about all the fun day trips and sexplorations when the boat docked at each harbor. Little did he know, I was terrified that my "cruise directing" would not take us to Pregnancy Island, as we hoped. I had thoughts like: *For goodness sakes, 16-year-olds accidentally figure this out all the time! If you can't figure it out, you're a loser.* Yuck! No one wants to have, and really believe, thoughts like that. But I did. When I thought I was Fertile Myrtle, I would tell my hubby, "It's go time!" and silently pray that I was right. I mean, all the signs were pointing to a huge ol' Las Vegas-style sign that said "FERTILE." But what if I needed glasses? What if the sign really said "FERTILIZER for Sale"? What if I screwed up? (Haha, get it?) If you saw a copy of my Taking Charge of Your Fertility, you would know that I battled this inner doubt. The cover is bent, the pages are worn. I used 500 highlighters in all colors to circle, underline and highlight the "important stuff" (everything in the book). I did not want to be the first person in the history of the world not to understand when it was go time.

Thankfully, I wasn't. All my temperature taking, highlighting, and cervical fluid observing paid off. I got all knocked up despite my worries that I didn't know how it was all going to come together.

I need to mention that it takes a varying amount of time for each couple to conceive. Please don't fall into the trap of comparing yourself and your journey with anyone else's. You may be a super fastidious temperature taker, know your cycle inside out and not get pregnant right away. Your journey may take longer than you'd like and involve consulting experts to help you and your partner navigate this road to conception. I really want to encourage you that if this is the case, please don't blame yourself; it doesn't mean you're doing something wrong. In fact, putting pressure on yourself to conceive may hinder your efforts. I know several friends who had trouble conceiving, adopted kids and then got pregnant! It's amazing how your body responds when the pressure's off!

I write this to illustrate the fact that you are captain of your fertility ship and doing a damn good job. So kick doubt's ass to the curb. Arm yourself with knowledge and smart, loving, encouraging people around you for support; believe in yourself and your ability to become pregnant and to give birth!

Signs You Might Be Pregnant

1. **You are one tired chick.** This can be an easy sign to miss, partly because many of us live very full, busy, scheduled lives. It's very easy to second-guess yourself and explain your fatigue away. For many women, the "I'm growing a human being in my womb" tiredness is literally a

tired like no other. You could sleep for days, wake up to pee and then sleep for another week solid and you would still feel tired. There is so much going on inside of your body that it's no wonder you feel sluggish. This is very normal and a good indicator that you might be pregs.

2. **You have the flu**. Okay you probably don't have the flu, but you think you do because you feel like poo. You're nauseous and may be hurling like a drunken sailor. You are in good company. According to the American Pregnancy Association, over half of women get morning sickness (which isn't limited to just the morning). Try eating small things more frequently. Having some crackers on your bedside table may help you first thing when you wake up. Make sure you're hydrated and that you rest. If things get really bad there is prescription medication that you can take or if all else fails, bitch about it. That always seems to help.

3. **Aunt Flow is late**. This may not be as obvious for some people since lots of women have irregular cycles, or maybe just got off birth control, etcetera. Rest assured though, if

you are with child, you can celebrate not dealing with Aunt Flow for a good long time! This is one of life's little blessings, considering the plenty of other happenings in your female region that more than compensate.

4. **Can't touch this!** Personally, one of my greatest joys in being pregnant (besides the actual little person inside me) was the fact that I could buy a new bra size for the first time since I turned 13. If you are blessed with an ample-sized rack, your blessings will grow to porn-star proportions, just wait. Sore boobages are another initial sign of pregnancy. They may be sore and ache and be really tender to the touch. This usually goes away after a few weeks and then you'll really start to notice the size changes. You may need to put signs on "the girls" that says, "Look, but don't touch" – at least for a bit.

5. **Urination station**. It's kind of funny that from the very start, pregnant mamas have to pee constantly. Going back to Anatomy 101, you might remember that your uterus is situated directly above your bladder, so pretty much

immediately, your uterus puts the pressure on your bladder as it starts growing.

6. **Cranky pants**. Your spouse might notice this before you do. You could feel weepy and really grouchy. You can thank the loads of hormones coursing through your body. This won't subside any time soon. Spouses: this is a fair warning: patience and empathy are greatly needed (in Costco sized proportions).

7. **Plugged up**. This is a lovely indicator of the baby growing inside you. Constipation. Remember those hormones we just talked about? Well there's one called progesterone which slows digestion and actually relaxes your bowels—so they really feel no urgency to get the poop out.

These signs are all good indicators, but what you'll need is confirmation of your suspicions. Pregnancy tests are 99% right on, if used properly. And of course, it's your prerogative if you want to buy a few different types just to be sure. If you do take the test and you get the "positive" or "yes" or "thumbs up" or whatever it is, you'll want to call your doctor or midwife to have them confirm what you already probably know to be true. Just to warn you, your doctor will want you to come in after you've missed a period. So it could be a bit before you get the thumbs up, confirming you're knocked-up-edness.

Now that you've seen the signs and taken the test(s), you're realizing that at this phase in your life, the things that were always considered "taboo" or "not appropriate for discussion" are wide open and inviting you in. All your bodily pieces and functions now have a new center spotlight in your life. Don't worry, if you insist that you will not be delving into these "gross" topics, rest assured that there are plenty of friends and strangers who will go there, and they won't be able to shut up about it, despite your best efforts and desperate attempts to make them.

I was waddling around Austin, 6 months pregnant and apparently had a sign on my baby bulge that said, "Come talk to me about anything." I was amazed how complete strangers at the grocery would approach me and tell me that I was having a boy (they just happened to be right), and randoms at the post office would give me baby advice. I'll never forget when I was out showing property (I used to be a realtor) and a man I had never met touched my belly and commented that my belly button had "popped." Huh? When in normal, non-pregnant life is this ever okay? Consider this a fair warning, bust out your mama ninja moves and prepare for the onslaught of awkward pregnant conversations with friends, family and strangers.

takeaways

- Start charting your temperature each morning and notice your cervical fluid to figure out when you're fertile.

- It may take longer than you'd like to get pregnant and may involve consulting a specialist. Remember that putting pressure on yourself can hinder your efforts.

- Your body will give you signs you're preggo. Take a test to confirm it.

- Once you're pregnant, your bodily functions might as well be front page news. Embrace this newfound openness.

two

I'm Pregs, Now What?

*A ship under sail and a big-bellied woman,
are the handsomest two things that can be seen common.
~Benjamin Franklin*

It was Christmas time and I was preparing to go to my husband's work Christmas party. My period was a bit late and I knew that we had tried getting pregnant a few weeks before, so before I went to the party and imbibed-took advantage of the free drinks- I took a pregnancy test. Hubby was still at work when I decided to do this. I took the test, not really thinking that I was pregnant at all. It was just a precaution against drinking copious amounts of alcohol in the name of merriment. My jaw dropped when I saw the double line. So much so, in fact, that five pregnancy tests later, I still could not pick my jaw off the floor. Steve came home from work and I immediately pushed him up the stairs to our bedroom and told him to take a look. He looked at the double lines and looked at me (my face shining bright with so much expectancy and joy that I was sure I was going to burst). He looked back at the double and looked back at me and said, "No way, holy smokes, no way, holy smokes, are you sure? Are you sure?" Of course, I cried and he did, too. Then I showed him my cache of the other five pregnancy tests showing that, yes, unless the makers of all 3 different brands of pregnancy tests were seriously jacked up, I was indeed one pregnant hoochie. But that's all I knew.

I had given no thought to the after. What happens after pregnancy is achieved? I had no idea what I wanted out of my birthing experience. Do you? "Um, hello Captain Obvious, how about a baby?" Well, of course you do, or why else would you be putting yourself and your womanly bits through this? Let's delve more into this topic of knowing what you want, shall we?

When I was in college and was in the midst of dating hell (wasn't a fan of the whole dating shindig), I heard a speaker talking about finding your mate. The speaker said something to the effect of—

> Imagine your life is a race. As you're running, take some time to look around you and see who you're running next to. Look over and smile and nod and maybe give a wave. Keep running. In a few miles, look over again. Is that same person still there? Are they running in the same direction, at the same pace as you are? If they are, give another smile, introduce yourself and keep running. It may end up that the race you're running is the same one they are; they could be your future spouse.

This really struck a chord with me. I wanted to marry someone who was running my race. The thing is I needed to know what was important to me. I needed to determine the vision for my future, my goals, my aspirations, so that I could identify if a boyfriend was running alongside me, or was veering off in a different direction altogether. I took the time and established a vision for my future. It just so happens that I did meet my husband in college, but at the time, we both evaluated our races and decided that we were going in opposite directions (I was heading to Morocco and Steve was heading to the Navy—very different races we were racing).Two years later, while I was running, I looked over and there Steve was! He was jogging—and so was I (actually, to be honest, we were kind of power walking, but that's just between you and I). I smiled and nodded and he did the same and we realized, after chatting, that we were going the same direction, the same route, the same pace. So we sealed the deal with a justice of the peace secret wedding.

But that's another story for another time.

The point here is this: knowing what you value, what you think, what you believe, what you want, and what you hope for during your pregnancy and birth is powerful. It allows you to find doctors, midwives, doulas, birth support, friends, neighbors and complete strangers who share the same race and can help make your journey sooo much more enriching and enjoyable. Don't believe me? Ask any woman who had a horrible birth experience because she didn't know what she wanted and settled for a doctor who accepted her insurance and nothing more. It happens. But it doesn't have to happen to you!

Here are some questions that you should take some time to think through. Now, take a deep breath and remain calm. You don't need to know all the answers to these questions right this second; you don't even need to know them today, or this week. Start thinking through them. After all, giving birth to a human being is a pretty big deal. Don't you want to make sure you do it the way you want?

1. **Big Picture**. From start to finish, how do you imagine your labor and delivery? Are you giving birth at home? At a hospital? At a birthing center? What are you wearing? Who is there with you? What is the ambiance of the room? Is there a birthing tub? Is there music?

2. **Specifics.** Now write down some specifics.

   a. How do you view the role of the doctor or midwife?

   b. Do you want your doctor to induce labor by 40 weeks?

   c. Do you want your body to naturally go into labor?

   d. Are you going to have an epidural?

   e. Will you choose to have this baby with no pain meds?

   f. Will you do perineal massage prior to delivery? Do you want the doctor to?

   g. Do you want to have an episiotomy?

   h. Do you want to tear naturally (if at all?)

   i. What position do you envision yourself giving birth in? On your side? On your Back? Crouching? In a birthing tub? Using a birth stool?

   j. Do you want to bring your own birthing ball?

   k. Will you hire a doula or other birth support?

   l. Do you want to be able to be free to walk around, hop in the tub or shower, and use a birthing ball during labor?

m. How many people do you want in the room with you?

n. Are you okay with a forceps or vacuum-assisted delivery?

o. What's your take on a c-section?

p. Do you want your baby placed on your chest immediately after birth?

q. Do you want your baby to stay in the room with you at all times?

Take some time to truly reflect on these questions. If you're not sure about what you think, that's okay, keep reflecting and reading, you will figure it out. Even if you're not 100% sure about some of the answers, it's great that you're thinking through these things.

Back to December of 2008 and the bomb that was just dropped. The most wonderful bomb called "newly impending parenthood." We were at hubby's work Christmas party, but not really. We were on clouds mostly. We kept looking at each other while we pretended to chat with people and kept smiling and having these fabulous non-verbal conversations, just the two of us. We decided not to tell our families...for five days. Those five days almost killed me- I tell my mom and sister everything the second it happens. But at the same time, it was so fun to have a secret that only Steve and I shared. We had that twinkle in our eye and that pep in our step.

I had the fabulous idea of making t-shirts to break the news to our families. Since we were flying home for Christmas and were to arrive on Christmas Eve, we figured out our plan. I made two t-shirts. One that said the word "Bun" in green letters on a white t-shirt that Steve wore. The other t-shirt had an arrow pointing down to a picture of an oven. We flew home, walked in the house and saw everyone. We were so excited, but we forced ourselves to chat and make small talk. Everyone was in the kitchen. Slowly we unbuttoned our button down shirts and took them off. We stood next to each other, doing the "middle-school dance" side hug thing. In slow motion, everyone's faces changed from "aww, isn't that cute?" to "whaaaaaaa?OHMYGOSH!!" It was so much fun! Mom started crying, grandma cried and of course everyone else followed.

Once the holidays were over and we got back home, we had to figure out what to do next. I had no idea. I had never been preggo before. Since we had recently moved to Austin, I figured I probably needed to find a doctor. So I spent, oh a total of 10 minutes doing that.

> "Hi, do you take 'such and such' insurance? You do? Are you accepting new patients? When can I set up an appointment?"

Done. I checked that one off my list, not realizing that my flippancy regarding this task would be one of my biggest lessons learned in my pregnancy.

Date Your Doctor/Midwife

The choice of your OB or midwife is potentially the most defining of your pregnancy. The reason? Your healthcare provider's skills, practices, beliefs, methods, and perspectives will directly impact your birthing experience.

Don't believe me? Read about a woman I'll call "Anna." This is part of her story:

> *"At about 24 weeks, my blood pressure went through the roof. I had never had a problem before this and had been at a regular visit when they asked me to go for some testing. I am a little on the neurotic side, so I bombarded them with questions because this was my first pregnancy. I was frantic and quite aware, by their behavior, that something was wrong. After hours of non-stress tests and detailed sonograms, they told me I had high blood pressure but the baby was okay and that I*

would need to take medication. After that I was in and out of the hospital on a regular basis.

At 28 weeks, they gave me steroids to develop my son's lungs. Not once did they tell me that I had preeclampsia, was high risk, or the effects it could have on my child. My husband kept saying we needed to trust our doctor.

I had to go for gestational diabetes testing and at 30 weeks it came back negative. He sent me again at 32 weeks and it was positive. Immediately, he put me on insulin. That worked for about 3 weeks. At 35 weeks, I began to simply not respond to insulin at all. They put me on rapid acting insulin to help. I had a severe allergic reaction. My body was covered in burning and itching hives and I could not breathe.

When my husband called, the nurse said I was overreacting and nobody had reactions to insulin. I went in anyway, because at this point I was so scared. I stomped in to L and D informing them they had 15 minutes to get my doctor or I was going postal. It worked. I hate to be a bully, but they responded to nothing else. My doctor said we would switch to another brand of rapid insulin. I refused. He said then we'd have to deliver the baby or it would die. I asked if I could just take another dose of slow acting insulin. He said no. I have 3 god-daughters and they were all preemies, so I knew the longer my baby cooked, the better. I asked to come home and that I would call if my levels got too high for my sugar. They kept me overnight, put me on fluids and sent me home. The doctor reminded me that I had asked to stick it out as long as possible. It struck me that I was being punished for sticking up for myself and my child.

I stuck it out two weeks— it was the strictest diet of protein, veggies and only water. My sugar was out of control but I just couldn't bring myself to tell my doctor. I didn't want my child born too early. I felt bullied. I knew there were risks to my high sugar, but I felt I couldn't trust my doctor. Not once did I think to change doctors."

Thinking back, it is more than a little embarrassing that I spent more time researching vacation destinations or what new vacuum I would buy, than I did figuring out who I was going to entrust the privilege of overseeing my prenatal care and eventually delivering my baby to. I cringe thinking back on that because I easily could have had the horrible experience that Anna had. Like so many women, Anna didn't realize that she was the one in charge and could hire and fire doctors at will. It would have saved her a lot of heartache to start out her pregnancy with finding the right doctor for her, someone who was on board with what she wanted for her birth and viewed Anna as a partner in this process, not someone to talk down to.

Look at finding your doctor or midwife as finding your soul mate. It may be a long "dating" process where you have to go through a couple of snoozer dates before you meet your ideal match, or it might be super easy and your first date reveals "the one." Regardless, you want to find someone who not only knows what they're doing medically, you want someone you gel with, someone who listens, understands your concerns, empathizes with you, someone who you feel comfortable with. After all, this person will likely be all up in your grill when you spread those legs and birth that baby. You should at least like and trust this person, right?

How to Find Your Doctor/Midwife Soul Mate

1. Talk to friends, relatives, co-workers or plain old strangers who are obviously pregnant (please don't ask people who look like they "may" be pregnant, this can be disastrous). Find out who they have as their OB or midwife. Ask them how their experience has been, if they like the practice and the hospital where they delivered or will be delivering, etcetera. Just as you would question and probe your future spouse, get answers, get details, my future mamas, it really matters!

2. As much as you love and respect your friends, family, co-workers and complete and obviously pregnant strangers, get online. Get the scoop. Google the name of the doctor(s) and see what comes up. It's as important to know the potentially bad stuff about the doctor as it is the good. Mamas have NO TROUBLE voicing their frustrations or their negative experiences, especially when it comes to the internet. You will usually be able to find forums where mamas discuss the doctor or practice and you can add your questions to the mix. This is a great way to get the whole picture. Also there are new sites where people rate the doctors like www.ratemds.com, or www.healthgrade.com, or www.angieslist.com. Even if you have to pay to find feedback, it's worth every penny. It may save you lots of stress, money, time and a bad experience. We're talking about your health and that of your baby, it's worth a few bucks to get the low down on doctors and midwives from people who have gone before you.

3. Call up the potential candidates, verify they do accept your insurance and are accepting new patients and ask to schedule a meeting with the doctor. Tell them you'd like to

spend 15 minutes getting to know them before you decide if they will be your doctor. In every other area of our lives, we have no problem making people work for our business. We get bids for roofing, plumbing, and yard work. We have potential babysitters come over to meet us and our kiddos before we allow them to spend time with our kids. We get estimates for car repair and remodeling jobs. So why in the world would we not get a feel for our potential doctor and make them really earn our trust and our business? It's important to make sure that the person who will bring your child into this world is someone who you trust, you have a good working relationship with and someone who respects your desires. After all, this is your birth, which happens to include a specific doctor, not the doctor's birth which happens to include you. You picking up what I'm puttin' down?

The First Date

So once you identify a few candidates, how will you know if they're "the one" to deliver your babe? Well, you're going to have to go on a first date. I know, I know. I hated the dating process. Getting all dolled up, setting super high expectations, having nervous first date jitters, showing up and wondering what he looks like, thinking about what on earth you'll talk about. I get it. First dates can be draining but they are critically important. Plus, these first dates will most likely be pretty short, doctors are usually busy (at least the good ones are), so you may only have 15 minutes or so with the doctor. Ask the questions that are most important for you. On my website (www.YourBabyBooty.com) I have a free downloadable question guide called "Make an Ask of Yourself" with tons of questions to ask yourself, your spouse, your prospective OB, midwife, pediatrician and doula. That should help get you started. I can't emphasize enough, how important this step is in finding the right doctor/midwife for you. If the doctor doesn't have time for you now, then maybe you shouldn't have time for them.

The One(s)

After your first dates with all your contenders, you're going to need to make a decision. Who's The One? This may be a difficult decision. There may be a few different doctors/midwives who you really connected with. Or, there may not be enough fish in the sea and you're not super stoked about any of the possibilities.

Don't forget that many women don't have their babies delivered by their main doctor or midwife. There's a huge chance that you will have another doctor or midwife in the practice who's on call. Not to get all *Sister Wives* on you, but you're going to need to check out the other doctors and midwives in the practice too by doing a speed dating type of scenario with them. Ask the doctor if the other doctors or midwives in the practice share the same approaches and beliefs as they do. This continuity must not be overlooked when choosing The One(s).

If you've really searched high and low and one doctor or midwife doesn't really stick out to you more than others, look at some secondary factors: at which hospital do they deliver? What have you heard about those hospitals and the birthing care by the nursing staff? Did you like the nurses and office manager at the doctor's office? Is it easy to get an appointment? What are the chances that the doctor will actually deliver your baby? Will you have a chance to meet the other doctors/midwives in the practice? What is their c-section rate? If the answers to these questions don't help you decide, then talk to your partner and see what their impressions are. Ask for a sign. Then make a decision and pat yourself on the back. You have just done more than the majority of pregnant women in America and you will be really glad you did.

The Break Up

As I mentioned before, I didn't do such a good job sussing out my doctor options after I found out I was pregnant. I am the queen of knee-jerk reactions. Pregnant? In five seconds I had my prenatal appointment made and checked off my list. I ended up going to a doctor who had been a doctor since before I was born. He was super qualified and a very nice man. He was rather old school in his approach. As with so many relationships, at the time, my zeal and enthusiasm about my pregnancy blinded my eyes to the fact that he wasn't The One for me. I thought that all doctors were created equal. I did ask a couple questions before I let him get all up in my grill -I'm not a total floozy. My biggest problem is that I didn't know what was important to me, simply because I didn't take the 15 minutes I am nudging you to take. I didn't know what my birthing experience could be. I didn't think it would matter that much.

It does.

My turning point was half way through my pregnancy when I watched a film called *The Business of Being Born*. I realized by watching other people's pregnancies and interactions with doctors, that I could have something better! Something more! Giving birth wasn't something to simply endure; it was an experience to embrace. It was an epiphany. While the doctor I had was competent and knowledgeable, we didn't connect at all. I thought back to the times when I would ask him questions and he would say, while not even looking at me, "it's in the packet of information I gave you." I mean, that was a glaring red light screaming for me to STOP! But I just zoomed on, blissfully unaware as to how cheated I was by not having someone who was really interested in me. Not just me as an incubator-with-child-type-person. Me, as a woman, a person who has feelings and opinions and a life outside the examination room doors. I'm not just a uterus with a head attached. I'm a person. This experience of pregnancy is intense, emotional and if it happens, it only happens once or several times in our entire lifetime-unless your last name is Duggar and then it happens like 19 or 20, I can't keep up. Having someone address those things when they talk to you is as important as the medical care they give.

I started researching and interviewing and found my Soul Mate. Well, actually it was Soul Mates. There are two doctors and three midwives in this practice. My first appointment was one hour. I was flabbergasted. The head nurse asked me all kinds of questions, she talked about diet, exercise, my past test results, thoughts on and approaches to child birth. I walked out of there and wanted to hug each and every person and let out a yipppeeee! I didn't know it could be like this! I felt nurtured and cared about. I felt as if there were no dumb questions and I wasn't wasting anyone's time.

It was marvelous. Then I gulped…crap. I forgot, this newfound relationship meant that I had to break up with my other doctor.

Being a self-respecting, confident person, I decided to do this dirty deed over the phone. I braced myself for the worst. I dialed up the practice, asked to speak to the doctor, and the bouncer, I mean receptionist asked what I wanted to talk to the doctor about. I told her that I was switching practices, that my needs just weren't really being met and that I had researched and found "…umm what? You need some paperwork? Oh a release? Um. Okay. Can you email it? I have to pay $25? All right, but I really just…tomorrow? Sure I can pick up my records tomorrow. Bye."

And that… was that. There was no crying, no pleading, no asking for second chances. I was a bit let down. After all, I was my doctor's pride and joy patient, right? Not so much. No one cared why I was switching, they just wanted their $25 bucks to make copies of my file and shuttle me out of their office and close the door.

That confirmed that I made the right decision.

Even if you're in the middle of your pregnancy and have realized that you're not with your Soul Mate of a doctor or midwife. It's not too late! I've heard of people firing their doctors AT THE HOSPITAL in the middle of labor! Just like you had to take charge of your fertility in order to get pregnant, you have to take charge of your birthing experience. Don't settle for second best! Go out and get it!

Nutrition

You're all set with your doctor and now is the time in your life when you start popping some prenatal vitamins and whip out that, "I'm eating for two" excuse. I hate to burst your pregnancy bubble, while it may feel like you need to eat for two because you're so hungry, in reality your little bambino only needs about 300 extra calories a day -that's a glass of juice and a hard-boiled egg. Sorry! You know those three hamburgers with bacon and cheese that you couldn't wait to get home to eat, so you stuffed yourself while sitting in the parking lot of the drive thru? Yeah, those were NOT because of the bun in your belly, that one is all YOU mama, all you. But it was pretty dang good, eh? Believe me, I've been there.

We've already briefly touched on the hormones coursing through your body causing a bit of crankiness. What those hormones also do is give you strange food cravings. One friend of mine is super into whole foods, healthy eating, healthy lifestyle stuff. While she was pregs, she couldn't eat a single vegetable. Well she could, but they were in the form of potato chips. After her baby was born, she magically snapped out of it. Hormones are the source of major food cravings and food aversions for pregnant people.

When I was in my first trimester, I experienced this phenomenon like crazy. It started with spaghetti and meatballs, accompanied by garlic bread. I was ravenous for this meal to the point that I ate entirely way too much one night and spent the next three hours moaning and in pain because I overate. One of my next cravings involved citrus. Citrus of any kind really and I didn't limit it to citrus, fruit of any color or variety usually hit the nail on the head. The big winner in the fruit category those few first months was grapefruit. I believe I single-handedly supported the entire crop of grapefruit that season. Those growers down in Florida were mighty thankful for my knocked-up-edness that year. Those sweet, juicy, citrusy fruits were just perfect for my hormone ravaged body. Of course I had the odd quick cravings for McDonald's cheeseburgers, or glazed doughnuts, but those seemed to lose their steam after one run.

There was one big craving however that led to a meltdown. We refer to it as the infamous "Fried Chicken Incident." Steve and I were at a store one weekend when I walked outside and took a big whiff of fried chicken and instantly HAD TO HAVE IT NOW! I told Steve, I want Golden Chick (fried chicken place). Being the reasonable, self-sacrificing, wonderful chef of a husband that he was, said "Great! I'll make it for you myself!" Well, how could I pass up on that offer? However magnificently sweet this offer was, I couldn't help but feel some druthers about this. Firstly, Steve had never made fried chicken for me and secondly, I was afraid it wasn't going to meet my expectations in terms of crispy, greasy, goodness. Well, suffice it to say, two packages of chicken tenders and two pounds of mashed potatoes later...I was bummed. I walked into the kitchen and there was not a crackling to be heard, nor a deep dish of canola oil in sight. I decided I had to step in and micro-manage, just a bit. The conversation went like this:

> Honey, are you planning on frying the chicken?
> -Yep.
> Well, don't you need a deep pan with oil in it?
> -Nope.
> Well, is this how your mother used to make it?
> -Yep.
> Well, will the skin be crispy and greasy and crunchy?
> -YUUUP.
> Okaayyy... as long as you're sure.

I have to mention the chicken was not as I had imagined it, though I'm sure it was tasty, it was entirely way devoid of fat and grease and crisp and crunch for my poor hormonal body to handle. I took two bites, gagged, cried and lay on the couch. Steve sat down—the conversation went like this:

>Honey, are you okay?
>- (snot, snot) Yup.
>Honey, are you crying over there?
>- (hiccup) Nope.
>Will you tell me what's wrong?
>- NOTHING'S WROOOOOOONG (sob, sob, sob, snot, snot, snot)
>Then why are you crying?
>-I DON'T KNOOOOOW! I know you've been trying to make me fried chicken, but it just wasn't the way I wanted it and I'm trying so hard not to be a brat and I appreciate you so much, but I just couldn't take more than two bites because I feel nauseous now...I'm so sorrrrrrryyyy!

I wailed for 15 minutes straight. And that, folks is a perfect example of pregnancy hormones in action—the new third wheel in your marriage.

Keeping some perspective about this whole nutrition topic, while it's important to eat healthy foods and get proper nutrition anytime, but especially when you're with child, it's also super important to cut yourself some slack and sometimes just give in to your cravings. You, your spouse and whoever else lives with you will be eternally thankful. And it will make this whole pregnancy journey a wee bit more enjoyable. Another healthy eating friend of mine felt so badly about her poor eating habits while pregnant that she decided to sneak in healthy super foods where she could. She would puree cauliflower and put it in her mac and cheese and then sneak some beans into her mashed potatoes. Very clever I tell you.

One last little tidbit about nutrition, you probably know this already but just in case you don't: start taking a prenatal vitamin. Studies have shown that vitamins such as folic acid and folates (part of the vitamin B family) have really reduced the risk of giving birth to a baby with a neural tube defect. This is particularly true while trying to conceive and during the first trimester. Leafy green veggies, oranges, and bananas contain folic acid, but taking a vitamin supplement will ensure you get enough.

Another thing I whole heartedly advocate is drinking lots of water. Not only does drinking water hydrate you, but it helps increase your blood volume and supplies your baby with necessary nutrients. Did you know that while you're pregnant your body temperature is elevated? This means it's easier to become dehydrated. Try to drink between 96 and 128 oz. of water a day -that's approximately 3 to 4 liters. If you're exercising regularly, that number should be at the higher end of that range.

Exercise

The U.S. Department of Health and Human Services recommends that healthy pregnant women get at least 2-1/2 hours of aerobic exercise every week. This works out to about 30 minutes a day, 5 days a week. If you've led a pretty active lifestyle, this may not be a big deal. If you haven't had exercise as part of your life, this is. Add into the mix the fact that you are super tired during your first trimester especially, and the last thing you'll feel like doing is exercising. This is where bribing works great. Tell yourself that you can stop and get an ice cream, or chocolate covered pickle (whatever it is that you're craving) or indulge in one of your favorite guilty pleasures, for me it's reality TV- I'm a self-confessed junkie, once you're done. It will do wonders for your exercise routine!

It comes down to this: giving birth to your baby is an incredible, athletic event. It will be your Mount Everest, your World Cup, your Ironman. You will be stretching your body (literally) like it's never been stretched before. Sure, your body is created to do this. Women have been doing this for centuries. But it helps to spend some time priming and preparing your body the same way an Olympic athlete prepares for their big event (don't worry, no pole-vaulting, speed skating or curling is required), in order to expedite your body's healing process after you give birth. There are a lot of things you won't be able to control during your pregnancy and birth; exercising, eating right, drinking lots of water and training for your birth are things in your control. So make a plan and do it mama.

Walk. The easiest and least expensive exercise option is walking. Go at a brisk pace so that you get your heart rate up. Bring some water with you so you stay hydrated and pick a route where there are bathroom options available. A good friend added to the mix will also help time to fly and before you know it, your 30 minutes is up and you're off to treat yourself to a splurge.

Prenatal yoga. Not only is it great exercise, but you will also meet other pregnant mamas at varying stages of their pregnancy. Prenatal yoga classes may also teach you techniques to help you focus and how to find your breath and also relaxation exercises. Who doesn't love to relax? I am a huge proponent of prenatal yoga because it really did prepare me for birth. I learned lots of useful tips and tools and I really felt support and encouragement from the women there. And gosh, of course my favorite part was the relaxation exercise at the end. My yoga teacher would prop my legs up and put lavender bags over my eyes and talk to us in this super calming voice. Just thinking about it now makes me feel relaxed. It's really crucial to nurture yourself through this process of giving life. So whether it's prenatal yoga, or prenatal massage, treat yourself!

Swim. When I was 9 months pregnant with our son, it was August, in Texas. It was a record-breaking summer for heat. We had 63 consecutive days of triple digits. Did I mention I was 9 months pregnant? Each and every day, I went to the nearest pool. Yep, I was that super pregnant lady, sportin' my bikini and my goggles. I swam and swam and swam. It felt great to be weightless and cool. Plus I was exercising my body and preparing my muscles for labor. And, let's not forget, providing some amazing eye candy for all the pool patrons (smirk).

Kegels. It was actually in my prenatal yoga class that our instructor told us that we needed to be doing our kegels like they were going out of style. For those who may not know what kegels are, just think about when you have to pee and you want to stop in the middle. Squeezing those muscles is what constitutes a kegel exercise. I had heard of them, but didn't realize how important they were in the process of childbirth and thereafter. Immediately after giving birth to my baby, I added the kegel to my "What people should really tell you but kinda forget to about giving birth" list.

You should be doing kegels 100 times a day. Why are they so important, you may ask? Kegels will strengthen the pelvic floor. Well I don't know about you, but I didn't even know my pelvis had a floor. But it does, I assure you. When our yogi said, "100 times a day," I didn't take her seriously. I thought she really meant like, 10. And I suffered the consequences. (I delve further into the Pelvis in Chapter 5, literally and figuratively.) My mother, a superstar Pilates instructor, recommends that women take the typical kegel exercise a few steps further by doing what she calls "elevator exercises."

{ Elevator Exercises Explained }

1. Sit, stand or lie down (wherever you're comfortable.)

2. Think about lifting up through your pelvic floor (like you would do a kegel) as if it's an elevator.

3. Lift your elevator as many floors as you can. Example: 1st floor, 2nd floor, 3rd floor, 4th floor. Take your time and think about holding the intensity and then squeeze even harder. Make sure you breathe as you lift your elevator.

4. Hold your elevator at the top (like a good chivalrous person) and then lower the elevator one floor at a time.

These elevator exercises are more intense and delve deeper than a regular kegel exercise and help develop core strength. My mama likes to say that these are "kegels on steroids." These elevator exercises are excellent for after labor, too.

Birth Support

As I was checking out the hospital where I was going to be giving birth, I noticed that the hospital website said that patients may bring their doulas with them. Immediately the first thing that sprung to mind was Obdula Oblongata, as in a part of your brain. OBVIOUSLY this isn't what they were referring to...I mean, of course all mothers bring their brains, pregnant or otherwise, with them to the delivery. My fast fingers quickly perused the world wide web and found that doulas are basically birthing coaches. Sweet. But why would I need one, I wondered? I was hoping that my mom was going to be there with me and of course, my husband. Then I remembered that anytime we go to a hospital, my hubby has the perpetual case of the heebie-jeebies. The sight of me in pain, having contractions and potentially swearing as I neared transition might be enough to send him into an alternate place...a place that wouldn't allow him to really coach me. So that would leave my mom, but then who would take pictures? I realized rather quickly the usefulness of a doula and decided to mention this to my husband to test out the waters:

Me: Hun, I was reading about delivery today on the hospital website, and they said we could bring a doula if we wanted.

Steve: What?

Me: I was reading about delivering the baby today, on the St. David's Hospital website and they said that we could bring in a doula, if we decided we needed one.

Steve: What's a doula? Is that like a Sherpa or something?

In case you're not fascinated with Mount Everest (as I am), you may not know who Sherpas are. Sherpas are indigenous

Himalayan people who have incredible strength, resilience and are considered to be expert mountaineers. These attributes make them invaluable guides when attempting to summit huge mountains such as Mt. Everest.

Hmmm...I thought to myself. Maybe a Sherpa would be the best option for us! After all, they are very strong (could pick Steve up when he faints), they have great resilience (I bet they wouldn't be put off by a woman screaming and potentially swearing while in transition), and they help people reach the top of the mountain (birthing a baby is a freaking mountain!). Perfect! My husband is a genius.

It turns out that Sherpas were in short supply in Austin, Texas at the time. But we ended up finding a doula who was wonderful. After our baby's birth, Steve said that having our doula was worth every penny -we paid about $600. He felt like he could really relax and enjoy the experience, knowing that we had someone who was trained in how to support us as a couple and could help run interference for us with hospital staff, if needed. Our doula gave my husband and mom wonderful suggestions on how to comfort me and also did things like get me ice chips and grab cold drinks for my husband and mom.

As with your doctor and midwife, selecting the right doula is an important decision and will require some interviewing skills. Go to the Doulas of North America (DONA) website and search for a doula in your area. DONA is the certification organization that I'm the most familiar with, so I recommend them. Call a few doulas and chat with them; you can tell a lot from just a phone conversation. If you feel like you click with them, then invite them over to meet you and your spouse. This meeting is usually free. Ask them lots of questions. I highly recommend choosing someone on the basis of your comfort level rather than their experience. There are fabulous doulas out there just beginning their doula journey and there are some not-so-fabulous doulas who have been doing this for a long time. Listen to your gut and to your spouse. Choose someone you both feel comfortable with. Remember, they're there to support you BOTH.

**If paying for a doula isn't in your budget,
I have a couple ideas:**

1. See if your parents or friends will donate to your doula fund in lieu of a shower gift.

2. Contact your local Doula Certification Organization like DONA and see if there is anyone who needs hours in order to be certified. Often they will act as your Doula for a greatly reduced price or even for free as part of their training.

takeaways

- Date your doctor. Just as finding a life partner is a process, so is finding the right person to deliver your precious cargo.
- Think through questions you want to ask your doctor.
- It's NEVER too late to break up with your care provider. Don't feel bad. This is YOUR baby's birth.
- Prepare your mind by doing mental toughness exercises and your body by doing yoga, swimming or walking for this amazing athletic feat.
- Hire a doula to support you and your hubby during labor.

three

Super Dad

What would men be without women?
Scarce, sir, mighty scarce.
~Mark Twain

Your body is changing rapidly, it's exciting, it's scary, it's fun, it's weird. Your hormones are adding some unpredictability to your life and your partner seems kind of oblivious to it all. The thing that's crazy about pregnancy is that there's a party going on in your womb and while you're the hostess with the mostest and you see signs of the party happening, there's a whole lot going on that you're blissfully unaware of. Eyebrows are forming? Baby is developing lungs? Baby can now hiccup? In many ways the party is going on without you. Imagine for a second how your partner feels. You're the one experiencing all these new found body changes, you can now feel the baby kicking for the first time (at least you think you can, it may be gas, you're not sure). Your partner is left out of the equation. Life for them goes on normally. They don't have any weird cravings, or extreme fatigue, their body isn't changing (or then again, maybe it is, but it has nothing to do with baby, it's more to do with you dragging him to Dunkin' Donuts at 10pm). For lots of spouses, reality really and truly doesn't hit until the baby is born. Then it's go time.

My husband is a pretty engaging type of fellow. He loves to be in the middle of the action and involved in whatever is going on. During my pregnancy, I felt really bummed out because I felt like he wasn't as excited as I was. Every single pound I gained, the moment my belly pooched out, the very second my boobs got larger, I felt like a walking billboard for "life change coming shortly." Steve on the other hand, didn't get it. If your spouse is researching baby equipment and registry suggestions and getting the email updates on your baby's weekly development, you are in the minority. Most women make the buying decisions for baby, and spend countless hours bleary-eyed looking at their computer screens, trying to figure out what stuff they need for baby. Which is the reason we started our website www.yourbabybooty.com, we want to help you mamas out with the mongo task of registering for baby.

After our son was born, my husband (who didn't seem very interested or concerned before) suddenly wanted to know about each and every item we had for baby. "Why did we choose this?" he would ask. And I would get pissed! Because *we* didn't choose it. I did! Then I would retort, "You surely didn't seem to care before... Why now?"

For my man, the pregnancy was real but didn't completely change his life. The second our little man came into the world, a light was switched on and being a dad and having a kid was suddenly very real and very wonderful. It wasn't that my husband didn't care about our baby stuff beforehand; he just didn't have a context to put it in. Steve needed to touch, to feel, to hold, to gaze, to watch, to behold this whole birth in order to be engaged. And once he saw it, he was all in. I had to remember that Steve and I are on the same team, we want the same things even though we often approach them from two unique directions and {newsflash}, I can't always get my husband to react the way I want, when I want. (My husband is peering over my shoulder reading this and wants me to repeat that, excuse me while I indulge.) "I can't always get my husband to react the way I want, when I want."

The first 3 months of your baby's life outside the womb is what I like to call "the man's pregnancy." Of course, his knocked-up-edness is a bit more abbreviated, potentially less uncomfortable and a whole lot more hands on. Once the baby is born, your spouse suddenly realizes the changes that accompany baby. Yes, you're still the rock star for giving birth and having a new little person to show for it and dealing with postpartum stuff. But hubby is now able to bond with the babe. Remember, your baby has been living in your body (what I like to call "the apartment") for almost a full year! You've felt him/her hiccup and move and roll over. You've been attached at the umbilical cord for a long time. Your spouse hasn't had this experience. Now is their time.

I had to get over my entitlement issues in order to help my husband feel like he was a part of this new life. I was exclusively breastfeeding at the time, and in hindsight, I think I would have pumped more so that Steve could have bottle fed our little guy from time to time. Not only would it have been a nice break for me, it would have allowed Steve some of those super special bonding moments, those times when you're feeding them and you just stare at their little face and watch them drink in the goodness of the milk. Yes. Those are some pretty sweet moments. Looking back, I was a bit stingy in this regard and should have been better at sharing. It is true that at the beginning, it's best not to use bottles and nurse at the same time, since the baby may get what is termed "nipple confusion." However, when you feel like your baby has the hang of things in the mammary department, throw in a bottle every now and then, it will not only give daddy a chance to bond, it will give you some freedom when you and hubby need a date night and babysitters enter the scene. But bottle feeding isn't the only way that daddies and babies can bond, here are some more suggestions.

Daddy Bonding In the Womb:

1. Ask him to slather cream on your belly and hopefully he will feel a kick or two while he's at it.
2. Ask daddy to go to your doctor's appointments with you, hear the heartbeat, and see the ultrasound.
3. Put him to work putting together the baby's bassinet, crib, or other assembly required items.
4. Suggest that he shop for or create a special gift to give your baby after he/she is born.

Daddy Bonding Out of the Womb:

1. Rock and roll. Daddies and babies rocking in a rocking chair are sure to result in some great sleepy time cuddles.

2. Since you just birthed this baby, and daddy (hopefully) has a few days off, ask daddy to be on diaper duty. There's nothing like some baby tar (meconium) to bond daddy and baby for life.

3. Bath time is a fun way to have special time with baby. Don't forget to cover the wee-wee if you have a boy, or daddy will experience a geyser to rival that of Old Faithful.

4. Don't forget that newborn, sleepy babies also need awake time, daddies can get right in there and play with baby so he/she is nice and awake after feedings (and you can nap).

My husband has often called me a control freak. I have no idea why. Giving him helpful hints on shortcuts and pointing out the occasional car (that he doesn't see coming) isn't really what I consider backseat driving. And it's certainly not being a control freak. If I was, then I would be driving all the time. Well this control freakish subject has become the proverbial pebble in the shoe of our marriage. Maybe it's because we're both (mostly) German (read: hardheaded) and have honest convictions about how we do things. I remember about 4 months into parenting, hubby wanted to have some father-son bonding in the form of bath duty. I was initially very pleased, because this afforded me 10 minutes or so of sipping wine all by my lonesome. For some reason - maybe there was nothing good on TV that night, or I didn't have a good book to read- I turned on the baby monitor, just so I could hear the bath time fun. It had nothing to do with the fact that I was spying on my husband, to make sure he was doing bath time "the best way" (my way). Of course my bath times were awesome. I would sing a vast array of bath appropriate songs, show tunes, etcetera. Songs like "…this is the way we wash your penis, wash your penis, wash your penis." You get the point. Back to spying, there was no singing happening, but there also wasn't any crying, either. Little Man and Hubby came downstairs a few minutes later all clean and smiling from ear to ear. My man was as proud as a mother hen. It was then that I noticed that our 4 month old baby was getting lost in his pajamas. Since I made a deal with my hubby and myself not to impose the way I do things on him and to let him figure out the whole parenting thing for himself, I let it go. Guess what? Little Man slept like a dream! Okay, that might be a bit of an exaggeration, but his awakenings in the middle of the night had more to do with losing his pacifier than having roomy pjs. The next morning as I was changing his clothes, I saw that the tag on the pjs read 9 months. I chuckled, took a few photos for posterity's sake and patted myself on the back for being okay with not being in control and starting to learn to go with it.

There are still moments when I cringe and bite my tongue, desiring desperately to change the outfit that doesn't match, or take over feeding duty, or giving helpful hints during bath time, but I'm learning to pipe down and let my hubby do his thing. He's an intelligent, pragmatic, resourceful, and (have I mentioned?) devilishly handsome man who doesn't need my tip of the day in order to make the world go round with our son. And in fact, when I do pipe down and chill out, I am the recipient of a super happy husband who is thrilled with discovering how to be a super star dad. The excitement, connectedness and bonding that we all enjoy as a result make it a huge win-win.

So I encourage you, before baby comes and certainly after, give your partner opportunities to be involved in the preparing, feeding, clothing, sleeping, play time of your bambino. The last thing you want to do is squelch any attempt on your man's part to find his own way of doing things. If you do, you might end up doing it all, forever.

takeaways

- Expectant papas need time to bond with baby, they can do this when the baby is in the womb, and after the baby comes out.

- Control freaks, let go and let your spouse BE.

- If you don't learn to let go, you may end up doing it all for the rest of time.

four

Tough as Nails

*The power and intensity of your contractions
cannot be stronger than you,
because it is you.*
~unknown

Developing mental toughness for your baby's birth is nothing to laugh at. Why do professional athletes work with trainers and psychologists on the physical and mental aspects of their game? Why do our military's elite forces like the Army Rangers, Navy SEALS and military pilots endure hours and hours of tough mental training? Because mental toughness directly links to success, and for our military's elite, successfully completing a mission is a matter of life and death. The mind is directly responsible for anything your body will ever do; train your mind to focus, to relax, to overcome pain and your body will be allowed to do what it does naturally.

Birthing a baby blows any other athletic event out of the water in terms of endurance, stamina, focus, concentration and intensity. Besides the exertion that women do externally, such as breathing through contractions, walking, squatting, sweating, and pushing, there's an incredible amount of activity going on inside the woman's body as she goes into labor. For example, a woman's body secretes hormones called relaxin during pregnancy which help ligaments and tendons loosen and stretch so the bones of the pelvis can expand to make room for baby. Researchers have found that labor starts when the baby's lungs secrete a substance that lets the mama's body know that baby is ready to be born and to release the oxytocin hormone to get labor going. And before you even go into labor your body is busy growing, feeding and nurturing your baby. Don't forget the milk factory in your bosom that is busy preparing colostrum and milk for baby which really kicks into high gear once labor starts. Imagine all this going on while you're blissfully unaware! No wonder some childbirth educators suggest that women could burn as many as 50,000 calories over the course of their labor and delivery. This sounds like an astronomical and ridiculous amount, but if you think about the fact that many women labor for hours upon hours in addition to all the things the body is doing to prepare for birth, prior to labor even beginning, it's plausible. But, of course, every woman's labor and delivery is different and so is the amount of calories burned.

Suffice it to say, giving birth is an incredible, athletic event and mentally preparing yourself to focus through the pain so you remain calm and relaxed while working effectively through each contraction is crucial. Yes. I realize that sounds asinine, but staying relaxed is key to getting that baby down through the birth canal and out of your body as efficiently as possible. Think how many mamas do it every day…you can do it, too!

Mental toughness is defined as an unshakeable perseverance and conviction towards some goal, despite pressure or adversity. As wonderful as all that sounds, mental toughness starts with attitude. Do you have a good attitude or a bad one? A positive one or a negative one? If you're hovering around the bad or negative vicinity, then you will definitely need to make some adjustments in your mental frame of mind. The authors of Mental Toughness: a Champion's State of Mind, write that the benefits of positive attitudes are:

✓ Enhanced optimism and positive expectations.
✓ High positive energy.
✓ Higher levels of confidence.
✓ Better concentration.
✓ Better decisions ('cause you're viewing possibilities instead of obstacles).
✓ Better learning.
✓ Greater determination and commitment.
✓ Greater happiness and peace of mind.

✓ Enhanced perseverance.
✓ A greater willingness to accept challenges.

Can you say, "totally applicable to birth?" The very same mental toughness and focus that athletes practice is the very same mental attitude you need as well. So, if you're not a naturally optimistic or positive person, how do you get there, to the land of positivity?

First one: Make the choice of being positive at all times. This may be difficult for you or it may be extremely easy; either way, make a goal of it early on in your pregnancy and know it is completely a choice you make.

Being positive comes naturally to me. I guess you can say that I'm a "glass is half full" kind of girl. Despite this fact, there were times during my pregnancy when it was hard to see the upside of the constant peeing or the tossing and turning at night or the fact that I had really bad lower back pain and could neither stand nor sit for longer than 10 minutes at a time. When I started feeling grumpy, I would focus on specific things I was grateful for. I would think about other women, friends of mine, who would have loved to walk a mile in my sometimes uncomfortable, pregnant shoes. That snapped me out of my negativity mode in a jiffy. It's ok to feel grumpy or even angry, it WILL happen, but channel those emotions back to the opportunity you have to give birth…it's so worth it!

Second one: Be aware of your attitude and constantly make the effort to understand your attitudes and motivations. Be honest with yourself about it. Once you're aware, you can squelch the unhelpful negative vibes as soon as they emerge.

I've already regaled you with the tale of my fried chicken meltdown. That story is a perfect example of realizing that what I was all broken up about (lack of greasy, crunchy, fried chicken) was silly and frivolous. I knew right away it was hormonal induced hysteria and had no other basis. I admitted it readily to my patient, empathic husband, which ended up helping him to respond to me in an understanding way. Remember that your spouse will be baffled as to why you respond the way you do, unless you communicate what you're feeling and why. When hormones or negative attitudes get the better of you, go ahead and admit it and move on.

Third one: **Stay away from negative people**. This is a big one. Negativity is pretty contagious. In fact, if you get together a few unhappy and negative people, a bitch session will unfold faster than you can say "happiness sucks." I'm going to go one step further and suggest that you find as many supportive, positive, optimistic people as you can while you prepare for birth. This doesn't mean that people are wearing My Little Pony t-shirts and twirling their hair while they skip down the street chasing rainbows. This just means that you have some people with good juju around you who will make like a good bra and uplift and support you (and your birthing goals) while adding some positivity into your life.

Now that you've given yourself an attitude adjustment, let's delve deeper into the specific practices and exercises to toughen you up mentally, which will exponentially help your ability to focus, relax and stay calm during birth.

In Psychology Today, Bakari Akil II, Ph.D. talks about how the Navy SEALS were having horrible fail rates for their training program. The heads of the Navy SEALS training program realized that the piece of the puzzle that was missing was mental toughness.

In one Navy SEAL test, the recruits are to stay underwater for 20 minutes using scuba gear. At first glance, this doesn't seem bad at all. (I loved it when I went scuba diving in Hawaii! I could totally be a Navy SEAL. Bring it on!) Well the instructors DID bring it on; they harassed the recruits underwater by tying up their air hoses, ripping off their masks and really pestering the snot out of them. The majority of the guys who panicked, failed that test over and over again (they were allowed 4 tries). The guys who expected the attack remained calm and didn't panic through the attack, passed with flying colors. The success rate all hinged on mental toughness. The higher-ups in the Navy decided to help these poor dudes out and start training them in four areas, so as to boost their success rate. These four areas are goal setting, self-talk, mental rehearsal and arousal control (ohhh! I bet you can't wait to get to that one).

Before exploring these exercises, I have to say that my husband has served with and knows many SEALS, and suffice it to say, they are some Bad Mama Jamas! If the already super tough guy Navy SEALS in training needed to add to their 'mental toughness' repertoire, then you and I can and should as well. These are techniques and exercises that you will use for the rest of your life in everyday situations as well.

Exercises to Develop Your Mental Focus

Goal Setting

Recruits were taught to set extremely short term goals. Goals like "I will survive until my next meal." These goals are achievable and we gain almost instant gratification from them, which really helps our mental perspective. In the arena of giving birth this could look like, "I will make it through my next contraction," or "I will make it until I get to the hospital," or "I will make it until I get my epidural."

How far?

Another way to look at it, instead of getting discouraged that you're only 4, 5, or 6 cm dilated think, "With every cm, I am one step closer to meeting my baby," and then visualize (more on that in a sec) meeting your baby in your happy place. Every painful contraction is one more contraction closer to meeting your baby. Every step, every bit of pain, every centimeter, every moment—you are one moment closer to meeting your child.

Self-Talk

There was a really fascinating program called The Brain on The History Channel and those super smart expert people remarked that we actually say 300 to 1000 words to ourselves each minute! Did you know that? The Navy SEALS taught their recruits to speak positively to themselves. By speaking to ourselves positively, we can actually override fear and anxiety which results from the amygdala (say what?), that's the part of the brain that deals with fear and anxiety. Remember how we were just talking about having a positive attitude? Now's the time when all your practice is put to great use. As you go through labor, speaking positively to yourself (or other people if you feel weird having pep talks with yourself) scientifically does make a difference in the fear or anxiety you feel, since it overrides the anxiety signal in your brain.

Mantras

It may be helpful to have a mantra you recite through your labor and delivery. It can be anything:

"I am a birthing warrior," or "If 'so and so' can do it, so can I," or you can even bust out, "you did this to me!"

I once read about a woman who opted for an un-medicated birth at home. It was a long and arduous labor and her mantra was "epidural, epidural, epidural." After her baby was born, she joked that the epidural got her through. If the word "mantra" sounds too scary or New-Agey for you, think about the fact that constant repetition can create a nice rhythm and really help you focus.

We have a very good friend who completed an ironman triathlon (swam 2.4 miles, biked 112 miles, ran 26.2 miles). Throughout the race, he used the mantra "long, calm, strong and smooth," which created a rhythm that forced his brain to overcome the pain signals he was feeling and helped his body to remember to take "long" strides, remain "calm" and controlled, think "strength" and be "smooth" on each and every exertion. If these caliber of athletes use this technique, do you think it applies to and will work for you? That would be a resounding "hells yeah" mama.

Blessed Strategy

Turn your mindset to the "Blessed" mindset. Saying or thinking to yourself: I am blessed to be pregnant and have this experience. I have the opportunity to experience giving birth and giving life to my son/daughter(s). There are millions of women who would kill for this opportunity and I am the one here right now with this opportunity! Focus on the blessedness of this experience.

Mental Rehearsal: Relaxation

Before you can use mental rehearsal to go through your birth, you need to be relaxed. At first glance, relaxing during labor and delivery seems ridiculous and unattainable. It's not. Sure, it's challenging and is a skill that must be practiced over and over in order to master it. Let's check out the Russians, who are a super example of relaxation. During the 1976 Olympics (before my time), the Russians won more gold medals than any other country. Of course, people speculated that their success was because steroids were being used. The Russian team, however, insisted that their success hinged on brand new training techniques—and mental toughness was the foundation with voluntary relaxation being one of the pillars.

When a person is deeply relaxed or even in a meditative state, studies show that brain waves slow down, as do heart rates, and respiration slows and becomes rhythmic—blood vessels in the entire body dilate, bringing a great flow of nutrients to the cells of every muscle. (Sounds pretty great, doesn't it?)

As wonderful as Russian Olympic athletes are, let's bring this back to you for a second. If you don't practice relaxation, you will most likely be tense, which will waste energy, make the pain more intense and will result in you getting fatigued faster. Relaxing your body will help the rest of your mental toughness, because it will calm your mind and will allow your body to get more oxygen, which decreases pain. One more big ticket item to this relaxation business—when you aren't all clenched up and tense, your baby will drop further and further into the pelvis since you're all relaxed in there. This is great news for your birthing self 'cause it means labor will progress faster than if you're all tensed up.

{ Relaxation Practice }

1. Find a quiet place (a walk-in closet will do).

2. Lay on your left side (put a pillow under your head and put a pillow between your legs if you want to).

3. Make a fist with your hand and squeeze it. Follow only your sensations and note the feelings in your palm and fingers. Take your time and notice each and every sensation and feeling. How does your clenched fist affect your breathing? Your neck? Your Back? Your shoulders? Do your legs feel tense?

4. Release your clenched fist. Relax your hand. Shake it gently.

5. Now go through each part of your body and decide to relax. Start at your toes, then your calf muscles, now relax your legs, let them sink into the ground beneath you. Continue with your abdomen and your hips, take deep breaths and imagine your body sinking into the floor. Relax your back—imagine your favorite masseuse is applying pressure to your lower and upper back, neck and shoulders. Breathe. Next, relax your hands, your wrists, your arms, drop your shoulders, relax your ears, let all the tension in your eyes be released and release any tension from your mouth. Take more deep breaths. Imagine yourself on your favorite beach, or in a hammock at your

favorite place. Breathe. Think about your whole body and sink even further and further into the ground below you. (Wow. I'm relaxed just writing this).

While I was in active labor, I had a tendency to tense my shoulders and my back. Our doula noticed this and directed my husband and mom to stand behind me and put their hands gently on my shoulders and my back. When I felt their touch, I immediately relaxed. It was nice to have their touch, rather than their voices telling me to relax. I can pretty much guarantee you that Birthzilla would have shown up if the phrase "just relax" was mentioned.

Practice partner relaxation with your birth support or spouse prior to your labor and delivery. When you're hanging out together, have them notice spots of tension and apply gentle pressure with their hand. See how your body responds. This will be a great, non-invasive, non-annoying technique when it's game time. Remember, relaxation is the first step to effective visualization.

Visualization

Dr. Loehr, one of the world's top sports psychologists, encourages the athletes that he trains to learn to picture things so vividly in their mind that they can actually hear, taste, feel and touch them. He writes in his book, The New Toughness Training for Sports, (Add LINK) that the brain is actually unable to differentiate between something vividly imagined from actual reality. So while it may seem silly to practice visualizing your birth before it even happens, rest assured you'll be in good company. Top performing athletes all over the world use visualization to mentally prepare for success. Golfing great Jack Nicklaus said, "I never hit a shot, not even in practice, without having a very sharp, in-focus picture of it in my head. First I see the ball where I want it to finish, nice and white and sitting up high on the bright green grass. Then the scene quickly changes, and I see the ball going there: its path, trajectory, and shape, even its behavior on landing. Then there is a sort of fade-out, and the next scene shows me making the kind of swing that will turn the previous images into reality."

Navy pilots train every day with substantial visualization techniques called chair-flying; they create dynamic and demanding flying scenarios before the flight actually occurs to ensure they are optimally prepared for the real thing. Talk about a great tool to use as you prepare to give life to this baby! Seeing yourself going through the experience beforehand, and imagining every detail, in a way becomes its own self-fulfilling prophesy.

{ How to Visualize }

1. Find a quiet place.

2. Close your eyes.

3. Envision yourself at the very beginning of labor. Maybe you're in bed and your water breaks, maybe you're at the mall and you lose your "baby cork" (you get the idea). Imagine each detail from what you're wearing to where you are. Picture your spouse coming home from work and telling him that you think you're in labor. Imagine counting the contractions and calling your doctor and your birth support. Think about deciding to go to the hospital and what that car ride is like. Maybe you're counting contractions or you're telling your hubby how to drive. See the hospital or birthing center (or home) and where you'll give birth to that baby. You're checking in to your room, what does it look like? What do you do when you get to your room? Your contractions are picking up in intensity; think about each contraction moving that baby down the birth canal. Where are you now? Are you sitting in the rocking chair? Maybe you're in the birthing tub. Are you listening to your playlist you made? The doctor or nurse just came in to check you, you have another contraction. Visualize your baby's trip down the birth canal, you're giving life to a human being. It's a miracle! See yourself pushing your sweet baby out into your world, feel the joy and happiness you, your family and friends

will feel. You're enjoying the sweet rewards of all your hard work, you're finally holding your baby, looking into his/her eyes. You're examining every toe, every finger. Your spouse and birth support are taking pictures. You notice that mass of hair and notice that your baby resembles your husband (of course!). You feel so happy and thankful that your baby is finally here.

Practice this visualization over and over. Even if your birth doesn't happen exactly like you envision, your brain will think you've experienced this before and will send signals to tell your body to relax which will really help you maintain focus and strengthen your confidence.

When the time finally arrives and you're in active labor do exactly what you've been doing this whole time. Visualize the miracle that's taking place AS you push, think about pushing that baby out into your world, the joy and happiness you and your family and friends will feel.

Again, it may seem silly to visualize all this, but mucho studies on peak performance confirm that visualization improves the desired performance outcome. This is a mandatory tool to have in your mental toughness toolbox as you prepare to give life to this baby.

Arousal Control

There is so much I could write about this, but I will not succumb to the pressures of my 6th grade mind and will stay on track (See? The power of mental focus is displayed). The Navy SEAL recruits were taught breathing techniques to help them take control of fear, anxiety and emotions that could really paralyze them. For birthing classes, this is the most commonly taught aspect of preparation, finding your breath. I found that I didn't remember a lot of what I was taught in my birthing class, but I did find my own rhythm and way of breathing that worked for me and I think that's pretty key for each and every pregnant woman. You have to find what works for you and go with it. Practice different ways of breathing. For example, long exhales in particular, mimic the body's relaxation process while deep inhales get more oxygen to the brain so you can function more effectively.

As a result of training the Navy SEAL recruits in how to manage fear and anxiety using the techniques discussed thus far, the pass rates went up one-quarter to one-third. Those are pretty stellar results.

If you're leery of all this mental toughness jargon and are feeling inhibited in your practice of these techniques, picture some tough guy Navy SEAL finding their breath, practicing self-talk and visualization. If the tough guys can do it, a birthing badass (that's you) can do it too.

Reward Yourself

I'm not saying that having a baby isn't a reward in and of itself. Having an external reward waiting for you after you have your baby can really help you get through rough patches, small things like your favorite meal, or a handbag you've had your eye on for months, or shopping for new post-baby jeans. Those things can be huge motivators to get you through rough patches.

I actually had several "rewards" for myself. After I had pushed my baby out, the first thing I wanted to eat was a glazed doughnut from Donut Taco Palace (don't ask). I think it's the best doughnut I've ever had. The next half dozen rewards came in the form of meals from the "outside." I chose to forgo my hospital meals and instead ate meals brought in by my mom and hubby. If a new pair of pumps or sweet handbag gives you that extra dose of determination to get this job done, then knock yourself out. Don't be afraid to use external reward to get you through.

Find Your Zone

The purpose of practicing all these exercises and working on your mental toughness is ultimately to get into your "zone." This looks and happens differently for each person. Essentially the world kind of slows down around you and you'll have the uncanny ability to hone in on certain things and leave out all others. There's a certain confidence that happens and an unshakeable conviction that you will make it and succeed. It's kind of magical. But it doesn't just happen because you want it to. It happens because you've practiced, prepared and trained your mind and body to optimally work together for the ultimate goal of birthing your beautiful baby. I had been in active labor for about five hours and my eyes were closed the entire time (except when I got up to walk or to go to the shower or change positions). There was no music in the room, only silence and the occasional voice of encouragement from my hubby, mom or doula. With each contraction I pictured a wave washing over me, bringing me one step closer to meeting my baby. I was so super focused on my breath that I literally had no idea what time it was, where I was, or what was going on around me. I was in my zone. After pushing for a while, the doctor asked me if I wanted to look down and see my baby coming out. I politely declined because I knew I still needed to focus on my job of getting this baby out. I did end up watching as I pushed the last push and it was a beautiful sight, one that I cherish forever. The point is that you may get into your zone through music or movement or through talking or laughing or silence. If you do think you'd like to have music to get you in the zone, make a CD or a playlist of some of your most inspirational music, it may be U2 or Beyonce, Lynard Skynard or Andrea Bocelli. When you're choosing music for your labor, think about the songs that really get you fired up and motivated, also think about the songs that soothe and calm you. Have a bit of both so you can have what you need, when you need it.

Getting in the zone is as unique as birth itself: it's different for everyone but it's helpful that you get there. When you're there it's like an out of body experience that will give you the oomph you need to birth your baby. Mental toughness is not for sissies, and woman, you aren't a sissy. So arm yourself and become a bad ass birthing warrior, because it's already in you, you just need a little nudge sometimes to bring it out.

Remember when we talked about vision for your birth? We want to be sure you didn't forget that part. (wink, wink, nudge, nudge) We all would agree that none of us can predict the future and our expectation should be that our birthing plan will change. So remember that by training your mind, you are training yourself to handle the changes that might occur during birth; you are NOT training yourself to expect one and only one type of birth.

This is important to understand. The mental toughness exercises train and prepare you for your birth experience, which might end up being different than the birth experience you wanted. Getting mentally tough and being prepared means knowing how to be focused YET flexible!

takeaways

- Olympic champions and our military's elite use mental toughness training for success and you as a birthing warrior should too.

- Make the choice to be positive; you ultimately control your mental frame of mind.

- Relaxation is key to effective visualization.

- Practice, practice, practice so you're ready for the real thing.

- Your "zone" happens when your practice meets game day.

five

The Gift of the Pelvis

"I don't like being called 'Elvis the Pelvis'. That's gotta be one of the most childish expressions I've ever heard coming from an adult."
-Elvis Presley

If you're anything like me when I was pregnant, I had no clue what a "Pelvic Floor" was. I thought it was the destination inside a medical building, not a place in my body. Let me just tell you that your pelvis and corresponding pelvic floor are major players in your ability to be pregnant, carry your baby in your womb, and give birth.

The pelvis is composed of four bones that form a circle; this is the opening your baby will travel through as you're in labor. Without getting all "Grey's Anatomy" on you, while you're pregnant, the wonderful flow of hormones coursing through your body will increase the diameter of your pelvis. Later, during labor, when your baby enters or engages the pelvis, the bones shift and the opening of the pelvis enlarges even more! Amazing!!

Perineum

The perineum, also known as "the pelvic floor" consists of two layers of muscles that are interwoven; they essentially enclose the bottom of the pelvis. These muscles form a sort of hammock for some verrrry important internal organs of yours: the bladder, uterus and rectum. These three fit together like a glove and hang out comfortably in the hammock of the pelvic floor. From the very start of pregnancy, your uterus will start thickening and will grow. By the 24th week of pregnancy, your uterus will probably reach just below your belly button. By week 36, you'll feel like your uterus is in your throat, but really it's just near your ribs and of course, by week 40, your uterus has overtaken your entire body -or at least that's how it feels and no one can tell you any differently. The ligaments that support your uterus adapt to these changes by stretching and shifting. The point in telling you all of this (besides the fact that it's super fascinating) is to tell you that your perineum needs some attention from you while you're pregnant. Remember in Chapter 2 when I explained how to do kegel and elevator exercises? Well, not only does your pelvic floor need to be strengthened prior to and after pregnancy, you will need to be intentional about protecting your perineum so you can avoid lifelong issues with incontinence, organ prolapse and other not-so-pleasant issues.

In addition to kegels and elevator exercises, there's another one you can do to strengthen your pelvic floor: squats. Squatting stretches the pelvic floor while also strengthening those quadriceps of yours, too. Be careful when squatting during your third trimester, as your ligaments are all loosey goosey and could easily be over-stretched; proceed with caution.

You can squat using a wall for back support, you can squat and lean forward holding on to a chair, or you can squat and use books under your heels. Squatting rocks and it's considered an ideal position for giving birth, too (thank you, gravity), ask your assigned nurse at the hospital to set up the squat bar for you (most beds are equipped with them).

A Different Type of Massage: The Perineal Kind

Perineal massage is another way to protect your perineum. This topic is something that our birthing class didn't even talk about at all, and many birthing classes don't, but it's so important. Why? Studies show that perineal massage may reduce tearing and help mamas to avoid the need for sutures or episiotomies during delivery.

Please just do me a favor, don't walk into a spa and ask if they do prenatal perineal massage. You'll get at least an eyebrow raise and a polite "not so much" from the receptionist, if she even knows what perineal means. Nope. You're on your own with the perineal massage, or you can recruit the willing hands of your spouse, since he will actually be able to see what he's doing.

{ Perineal Massage 101 }

1. Wash your hands (make sure you don't have any sharp, long nails. Ouch.)

2. Get some cold pressed oil (like olive oil)

3. Locate your perineum/ your central tendon of the perineum-the area above your anus and below your vaginal opening, apply some oil there. (see illustration)

4. Put the oil on your thumbs and slide your thumbs up your vagina (to the first knuckle).

5. Make a "u" shape movement with your thumbs- gently stretching the vaginal opening.

6. Repeat.

The muscles that form your pelvic floor criss-cross, weave and interlace and basically merge at a point that's called the "central tendon of the perineum." This is basically the anchoring point for the surrounding muscles. As I outlined above, this point is located right above your anus and right below your vaginal opening. As you can probably imagine, when your baby's head crowns, this area is under a tremendous amount of pressure.

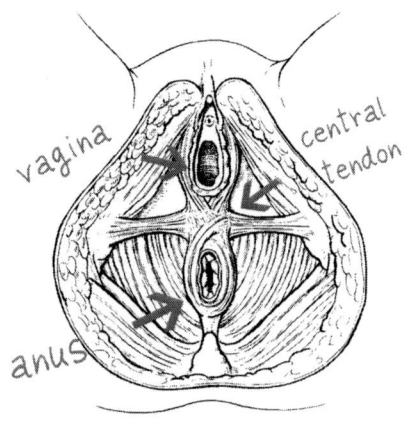

Three things could happen during delivery:

1. You deliver your baby and you have no tearing at all. This may be due to the steps you took to protect your perineum, your baby's head size, slow controlled pushing or sheer luck.

2. During your baby's birth you tear naturally, even if you took steps to protect your perineum.

3. Your doctor does an episiotomy. An episiotomy is an incision made with surgical scissors to the perineum which

makes the vaginal opening bigger (instead of tearing naturally).

In the past few decades, the routine use of episiotomies during childbirth has declined. Perhaps one of the reasons is that research shows that natural tears are actually less severe than episiotomies. Regardless, before you go guns a blazin' with your pushing, it's a good idea to do a couple half pushes when you are ready to push, so you can "warm up" your perineum and hopefully avoid or lessen the tearing. You can also ask your doctor or midwife to use olive oil to massage your perineum as you push (literally, on our itemized hospital bill, there was the most expensive bottle of olive oil ever!)

There are two additional things you can do to protect your perineum before you start pushing.

1. Soak in a warm (not hot) bath for 15 minutes to a half hour. This usually helps the perineum become more supple and relaxed.

2. If a bath isn't a doable option, you can achieve similar results with a towel soaked in warm/hot water and wrung out -think spa facial. The warmth and humidity applied to your perineum will also help it to become more pliable.

Due to hospital rules and regs, you may not be able to do the two things above once you're checked in, but you can always ask your doctor ahead of time so that you can make sure to do this at home before you are admitted to the hospital.

If you tear or have an episiotomy, the doctor will need to stitch you up after the baby has come. They apply a local anesthetic and give you sutures. You may read this and think, "great another thing to look forward to." Trust me on this one, after pushing a baby out of your body, you will be so overcome with adrenaline, endorphins and sheer bliss that you probably won't even notice what the doctor is doing down there. BUT, having said that, your doctor MUST perform those sutures in the correct way, if they don't, you may have problems with incontinence and other more serious problems for a long, long time. This goes back to the "doctor dating" scenario: ask lots of questions before you hire your doctor and talk to people who have used your doctor or midwife!

Time to Poosh!

By the time I reached 10 centimeters, I was desperately ready to push and it wasn't necessarily because I felt the urge to push but because I wanted our baby out of my body! My doctor instructed me to do some half pushes (to warm up the perineum). When she finally gave me the green light to "for real push", I couldn't figure out how to do it! I was using up tremendous amounts of energy trying to figure out how to push effectively and it wasn't happening. I had probably been pushing for 20 minutes or so when the doctor had to give me the smack down. She said, "Stop. Relax your face. You are wasting precious energy by squinching up your face and making all your grunting noises." She touched my hoohaa and said, "do you feel this?" I said, "uh huh." She responded, "When you push, push my fingers." Now I understand why she said what she did, I had no idea at that time that I could actually push in the direction of my vagina, or my anus. I was pushing towards my anus which wasn't helping at all, and in fact, could really have done some long-term damage. If you ask friends of yours about pushing, I venture to say that many of them will say that pushing was more difficult than they thought it would be, and I completely agree. But it doesn't have to be that way.

Did you know that those of you who don't get an epidural can decide when you want to push? More often than not, having a nurse telling you when and how long you can push interferes with the rhythm of labor that you've created and can be extremely distracting. After your care provider makes sure you're completely dilated, you can start pushing during contractions, or in between contractions. I've read about women who have reached 10 centimeters and didn't start pushing for another hour-they waited until they felt the natural urge to push. The best way to push is to push according to how you naturally feel like you should do it. I'm convinced that had I listened to my body and started pushing when my body told me to, Jackson was so low that I would not have had to push for 45 minutes and I doubt I would have torn as badly. Tears are measured in degrees, mine was a second-degree tear. Lesson learned for me. Remember, your body knows how to birth this baby, listen to it, follow it and remain patient with the process!

There are 2 ways you can push:

1. Pushing while holding your breath. Most of us, when we think of pushing, we think of pooping. It's not glam, it's not purdy, but it's true. In fact, some doctors will say, "bear down like you're having a bowel movement." This may be the only thing that we can immediately relate to, but saying that often confuses us and forces us to misdirect our pushing efforts.

Pushing while you're holding your breath, also called directed pushing or purple pushing, because your face turns purple (nurse is usually counting) is a forceful push. Directed pushing will produce quicker results (i.e. getting baby out faster) but you have to proceed with caution, as pushing too hard, too quickly, before your perineum has a chance to warm up, can cause major tearing. When you hold your breath and bear down, you're engaging your diaphragm, which gives you extra power, but at times, it could be too much. As you push, imagine your pelvis, your pelvic floor, and your baby traveling downward and out into the world, picture your vaginal opening and direct your pushing towards your vagina, not your anus.

2. Pushing while breathing through the push. Pushing while you breathe is a gentler push and won't produce quick results, but it's a great way to protect your perineum while making headway (excuse the pun) and getting baby out. You may decide to use a combination of both #1 and #2. While you're doing this type of pushing, you essentially focus on the same point (your vagina) and push in that direction. As you bear down, you breathe, or sigh, or moan through it,

which actually disengages your diaphragm and lets your uterus and your rectus abdominis (lower abs) do all the work.

The pushing practice that you can do is really more mental in nature. You don't want to practice "for real" pushing—i.e. pushing towards your vagina—until it's game time. Instead, by being familiar with your womanly bits and pieces, knowing what your perineum is located and the difference between pushing towards your anus and pushing towards your vagina, you will really be ahead of the game when it is time to push baby out.

You can practice the breathing through your push when you're on the toilet doing your business- just make sure you aren't pushing towards your vagina. I can't stress this enough. You don't push towards your vagina until it's really time to push baby out. Being in touch (literally) with your perineum and your body's anatomy will really help you to push more effectively. For those of you who will have an epidural, this is especially important since you (most likely) won't be able to feel what you're doing as you push, you'll have to visualize it. This intimate knowledge of your body will be a huge advantage.

takeaways

- Protect and serve your perineum by doing these things:
  - ✓ Perineal massage
  - ✓ Warm bath/warm compress
  - ✓ Do warm up pushes, or breathe through your pushes
  - ✓ Talk to your doctor about episiotomies and perineum protection PRIOR to d-day.

- Kick up your pelvic floor strength a few notches by doing:
  - ✓ Kegels
  - ✓ Elevator exercises
  - ✓ Squats

six

Decisions, Decisions

*Yesterday is gone. Tomorrow has not yet come.
We only have today. Let us begin.
- Mother Teresa*

After I found out that I was pregnant, my mother (a former hippie) asked me if I was going to use drugs during my birth. My answer was a resounding, "Hell to the Yes!" I reasoned that God created people who created magic drugs like epidurals for a purpose! Why would I ever suffer through childbirth, like freaking Laura Ingalls Wilder, if I didn't have to? Well, I did end up changing my tune on that song (much to the delight of my au naturel, hippified mama). The point I urge each of you to consider is that of taking charge, once again. You need to consider having the birth that YOU really want and not just going with the flow and being a passive participant in the birthing process. There are enough things that happen in the journey to the MotherLand which are completely outside your control, so knowing what you want and really advocating for yourselves and your choices (which are hopefully informed ones) is really a right, not just a privilege. To borrow a quote from the think tank known as The Beastie Boys, "You've got to fight…for your right…." Get my drift?

The Epidural

According to the American Pregnancy Association,

> "Epidurals block the nerve impulses from the lower spinal segments resulting in decreased sensation in the lower half of the body. Epidural medications fall into a class of drugs called local anesthetics, such as

bupivacaine, chloroprocaine, or lidocaine. They are often delivered in combination with opioids or narcotics, such as fentanyl and sufentanil, to decrease the required dose of local anesthetic. This way pain relief is achieved with minimal effects. These medications may be used in combination with epinephrine, fentanyl, morphine, or clonidine to prolong the epidural's effect or stabilize the mother's blood pressure."

This is an opportune moment to remind you to discuss this stuff with your doctor prior to d-day. Do you have known allergies or aversions to any of these medications? If you do, your Birth Vision (also known as birth plan) will likely be affected. If you're not sure, ask your relatives about any history of reactions or allergies in your family tree.

Should you choose the epidural route, here's a brief synopsis of the procedure:
The first thing that will happen is you will be given fluids via an IV. After that, the anesthesiologist will come in and will give you a local anesthetic on your back (so you won't

feel the next part). Then a needle goes into the numbed area in the lower back (along the spine). A small tube (what is referred to as a catheter) is threaded through the needle into the epidural space in your spine. The needle is removed and the catheter stays put so that the pain meds can be given periodically or continually, depending on what YOU decide. This is another great talking point between you and your doctor prior to your labor. The catheter will be taped to your back to prevent it from slipping out. Depending on many different factors, such as how your body responds, the type of epidural and the dose, you will either be numb from the top of your uterus to your pelvis or even from your chest down. Some women don't feel much pain relief at all. It all goes back to your medical history, and how you respond or react to the different meds. This is another reason why it's important to prepare for birth as if you weren't going to use meds at all. You don't know what will happen and being prepared is your biggest asset in having a birthing experience with no regrets.

There are, of course, advantages and disadvantages to using epidurals.

Advantages for You

- If you have a long labor and are getting tired, an epidural provides you with relief and the chance to get some rest so that you have enough "oomph" to push the baby out.
- 98.8% of mamas who receive epidurals receive significant pain relief.

Advantages for Your Baby

- There (honestly) aren't any.

Disadvantages for You

- When you get an epidural, you will also be attached to an IV so you can get fluids. You'll also have a bladder catheter (so you can do your business) and your blood pressure, the baby's heart rate and contractions will be continuously monitored.

- Because you won't be able to feel the lower nether-regions of your body and thus won't be able to move, you will be confined to your bed.
- You may feel nauseous and start throwing up. Tossing your cookies will deplete your body of the needed energy to finish your job of getting baby out.
- Drop in blood pressure (hypotension) can result in a decrease of the blood supply through the placenta to the baby and cause them distress.
- Labor will slow down after an epidural. The reason for this is that the medicine in the epidural essentially weakens all the muscles (that are now numb) which lessons the strength of the contractions.
- Pitocin (synthetic oxytocin) will be administered to speed up the labor which will actually make your contractions more intense than you would have naturally. While you will be blissfully unaware as to how strong your contractions are, your baby will feel them and may not be able to tolerate the strength and could experience distress, which may lead to a c-section or forceps or vacuum delivery.

- It may take a while for the meds to wear off after the birth, so you may have to have assistance to get around.

Disadvantages for Your Baby

- The epidural can cause your baby to have an abnormal heart rate.
- Pitocin will cause the baby to experience very intense contractions which may cause them distress.
- Your baby will most likely be drowsy at birth (remember what you put into your body also goes to the baby), this sleepiness can impact their sucking reflex, making it weak.
- Baby also may have poor muscle strength or tone in the first few hours which could lead to them being taken to the nursery for observation.

Other Medicines

Other forms of pain medications sometimes used during birth are narcotics, local anesthetic injections, pudendal blocks, and tranquilizers. We're not going to go in depth with these. Definitely talk to your doc about these other pain medication options.

All of this information can be a little daunting. Okay, a lot. Think about your soul mate, ya know your doctor/midwife who you hand-picked to help you navigate this jungle? Yes! Talk to them about all this stuff. Ask them about the things that concern you and remember that your doctor cannot read your mind. Inform your doctor about your history, and your particular situation so that he/she can really give you the information that is especially pertinent for you.

The Un-medicated Birth

Okay, so if you're a preggo person who is in the "hell to the yeah I want drugs" camp, you may think you can skip this section. And you would be wrong. Yes, I know that you are opting to take advantage of the wonderful blessings of man-made painkilling medications. BUT (and it's a big one) there will still be some pain involved in the bringing of this precious human being into the world.

So here's the scoop. There are a lot of ways this whole labor thing can go down (pun intended) so many ways that we can't even begin to discuss. Your labor could be super long, it could be super short, or it could be an average length. No one knows (except for God) what your labor will be like until you're there. Most likely, there will be a time when you are at home dealing with contractions and your doctor says, "Wait to come in to the hospital until your contractions are 5 minutes apart, lasting for 1 minute and this goes on for 1 hour." That means you are at home without your epidural. It is also possible that your labor hits you like a Mack truck and you are minutes away from being the top news story about a woman who had to drive herself to the hospital while giving birth in her car on the highway—because your labor came on so fast. Suffice it to say that your "ideal" birth may not happen and being prepared to deal with pain is a really good idea.

Advantages to an Un-medicated Birth:

- Having more control over your body and your environment, i.e.: changing positions, freedom to move around, using the shower, birthing tub, or other resources.

- Feeling empowerment and a huge sense of satisfaction/euphoria after the birth. I'm not being overly dramatic. I'm convinced you will always look back and realize this was one of your biggest accomplishments in your entire life.

- Usually a quicker recovery time.

- There are no "side-effects" or "risks" associated with an un-medicated birth.

Disadvantages to an Un-medicated Birth:

- Pain. It will hurt. Don't let that scare you away; it's manageable, it's doable, your body was designed in incredible ways to make this happen. You'll be in good company; thousands of mamas do it every day, all over the world!

- Negative feedback. When you tell people that you plan on having a "natural" or un-medicated birth, prepare for some negative responses and people shaking their head wondering why you would ever "do this to yourself." This isn't necessarily a disadvantage, but a reality for lots of people. So charge on ahead, mama, and let them know that your badass birthing warrior self is ready to do what your body is made to do.

What it all boils down to is that you've got some decisions to make. Some very important ones. That's why the dating your doctor and finding your soul mate is such an integral part in this process. You need to find a healthcare provider who is down with your vision for your birth. Someone who supports you in this birth process, whether or not you choose the medicated or un-medicated route. It's crucial that your healthcare provider, your spouse, and your birthing support are all on the same page with the decisions that you have made about what you want for your birth. It's that simple.

takeaways

- Take the time to consider the risks to you and your baby of a medicated birth.

- Explore the un-medicated birth option.

- Figure out which way of birthing is the best for you and your baby.

seven

Is It Go Time?

Adopt the pace of nature: her secret is patience.
~Ralph Waldo Emerson

If you find yourself confused as to whether you're experiencing "real labor," join the club. Many women experience Braxton Hicks contractions for weeks leading up to the birth of their baby. In fact, Braxton Hicks contractions can start as early as 6 weeks, but they can't usually be felt until much later in pregnancy. These contractions are infrequent, irregular and don't cause much, if any, pain.

Prodromal Labor is early labor and the body's way of getting ready for the real thing. The contractions that accompany prodromal labor don't help the baby's birth to progress, but they usually do get both the women and men's hearts' pumping and lure them into thinking that "baby will be here any second." Knowing when active labor really, truly is happening is rather confusing because of the uniqueness of labor for each and every woman.

Four Signs of Early Labor:

1. Rupture of Membranes (your water breaks)- though for some, the water doesn't break and the baby is born "in the caul." This is pretty rare these days since lots of health care providers do break the waters. Basically you can be in labor without your water breaking.

2. Losing the mucus plug—this is what seals up the cervical opening while you're preggo.

{Side note: What genius came up with the name "mucus plug"? I gag. I propose the term "baby cork" instead. Much better.}

3. Bloody show- while this sounds like something a British rocker would say about a recent performance- it's not. Bloody show is way less sexy, consisting of blood tinged mucous.

4. Mild contractions

Pam England writes in her book, Birthing From Within that "A watched kettle never boils…and a timed uterus never contracts." She goes on to say that women and spouses should ditch the time keeping techniques and get immersed in the experience of labor so that the woman's uterus will not have performance anxiety by being so closely monitored.

Especially for those pregnant for the first time, the early, mild contractions -which get your cervix ready for active or hard labor- can go on for hours or a full day. Women usually have a burst of energy that happens right before labor begins. Use this gift of momentum to complete tasks that you probably won't get to for a while after baby comes. For example: finishing a photo album, doing laundry, making some post-baby meals and freezing them, writing thank you notes, paying bills or baking cookies.

You'll be burning lots of calories while you're in labor, so while you're in early labor at home, drink lots of fluids like Gatorade, Recharge or cold juice, another great option is raspberry leaf tea which can be consumed hot or cold- it helps tone the uterus among lots of other things. Also make sure to eat small things like fruit, yogurt, cereal, toast, etcetera. You'll need the energy when you hit active labor and once you're at the hospital, most won't allow you to eat or drink (in case of emergency c-section) until your baby is born. So eat and drink up while you still can!

Most health care providers and birthing classes will tell you that when you reach 5-1-1, it's time to go to the hospital/birthing center.

> 5- Contractions are 5 minutes apart.
> 1- They last 1 minute.
> 1- This continues for 1 hour

Other experienced birth professionals will advise women to stay at home as long as possible (it's more comfortable there and you can eat, drink and move around at will) and to go to the hospital when the contractions get intense enough that you can no longer focus on anything else but your labor (i.e. your cookies start to burn). Now might be a good time to bust out your stop watch and figure out how long contractions are lasting and how much time you have in between since you'll have to let your doctor or midwife know. Stay in close contact with your care provider as contractions become more intense.

One last piece of advice, when in doubt, go. You will not be the first nor last couple to go to the hospital, get checked, and return home. If you're feeling anxious and feel like you really need or want to be there (at the hospital), then call your doctor and head on over. You may have an easier time progressing in labor if your mind is at ease, and for some, that means being at the hospital- for others that means staying at home as long as possible.

takeaways

- Figuring out if you're really in labor can be confusing.

- Ditch the stopwatch and let your uterus do its thing; it may get stage fright and stop contracting if you obsess about it.

- Make sure to hydrate and eat small bites throughout your early labor, you'll need the energy later.

- 5-1-1 go to the hospital or wait until your cookies burn.

- When in doubt—go. You can always come home if it's a false alarm.

eight

Keep the Party Going

*Endurance is nobler than strength,
and patience than beauty.
~John Ruskin*

In a perfect world, you go into labor while progressing at a good speed. Sometimes though, it's like starting a lawnmower that is low on 87 octane gas. You rev it up, get some gumption and then the mower sputters and dies. Maybe it needs more gas enhancer or whatever that stuff is called. So you add some enhancer, make sure to prime it a few times and pull the cord. It starts, lets off a few puffs of smoke into the air (that's you verbally venting) and then sputters again. You get the picture. Labor can often be that way. Welcome to the club, it happens.

I was one of the 12% of women whose water breaks prior to going to the hospital. It broke at 2:00 am and nothing happened for hours and hours. No contractions, nothing. I had lost my baby cork a couple days before, so I was seeing little things starting to happen but no major or minor contractions to speak of.

I thought about all the TV shows that I had watched that portray a pregnant woman going into labor. Her water breaks, she frantically rushes out of the house like it was on fire and then baby is born five seconds later. So understandably, I was all jazzed thinking that contractions would really get going and our baby would be born imminently. Well, if "imminently" meant 25 hours later, then I would've been correct. Clearly, my experience was not made for TV. I spent the next 18 hours trying to get labor moving because it wasn't happening. Both my doctor and my doula (or birth Sherpa, as my husband likes to say) told me to stay active- no eating munchies on the couch for me.

If you find yourself in the position of a seemingly stalled labor, the important thing is to stay active as much as possible. Even a little activity forces your body to move, which helps your mind to think about moving and the next thing you know, the Mayflower Truck has shown up and is moving that baby out of the womb and into your arms.

10 simple suggestions to keep the labor party going:

1. Are you well hydrated? Drink lots of water and also consider drinking something like coconut water (naturally contains electrolytes) or Recharge (an organic sports drink). Oftentimes stalled labor gets cranked up into high gear once the mama drinks some fluids. The uterus is like any other muscle, being adequately hydrated will ensure that it works properly. Think about the fact that marathon runners have hydration stations along their route. Replacing lost electrolytes will help you and your uterus function more

optimally. If you're feeling thirsty, your body is already dehydrated; stay on top of your fluids.

Note: conversely, dehydration can cause preterm labor.

2. Do stairs. When I say "do," I mean "climb." Go up and down as much as you can handle.

3. Use a birthing ball. A birthing ball is nothing more than a simple abdominal exercise ball that you may have somewhere in your basement or extra closet. Sitting on the ball and rocking back and forth can really relieve a lot of pressure on your pelvis and the rocking motion opens up your hips so that the baby can (hopefully) dip lower and lower into the birth canal. The birthing ball was my best ninja secret weapon birthing tool. The reason? There are countless ways you can use it during labor and it was heaven to sit on.

4. You can try walking, which is another activity that helps labor progress. Since I was 9 months pregnant during the

hottest part of the summer in Texas, we headed for our local mall and joined quite a few other people who were doing their mall laps. Mind you, most of them were over the age of 65, but the AC combined with taking short breaks in front of oh… GAP Baby, makes it a very worthwhile activity.

5. Squats are a great exercise to do when you're preparing for birth, and if you've been doing them because they help prepare your pelvic floor for labor, definitely continue. If you haven't done a single squat your entire pregnancy, now probably isn't the time to try them -sore muscles.

6. If you've been lying on your back having contractions, try lying on your side. Lying on your back can prevent optimal blood flow to your uterus since the baby is essentially squashing the major arteries that provide the blood flow to that area. Aside from that tidbit of info, sometimes simply changing positions will make a huge difference to the speed of labor. Variety is the spice of life mamas!

7. Get in the shower. You can sit on a birthing ball (if the shower is big enough) and let the warm water run down your back. This not only may help labor gain momentum, it might feel really good and help you relax (another one of my ninja tips).

8. Put the birthing ball on the bed, get on all fours on the bed put your arms around the ball (with your forehead on the ball). Some balls come with covers, or you can use a towel or blankie so that you don't slip or stick when you're sweaty. This may be a good one for you as contractions pick up their speed and intensity. There's honestly no rationale for why this might feel good; it either will, or it won't. You have to try lots of different positions and see which works best for you.

9. Grab your birth partner and face them as if you're dancing, put your arms around their shoulder and put your head on their neck or chest and sway or move. Swaying and rocking can help get you into a rhythm which can help with breathing and pain management.

10. Most hospital rooms have a rocking chair; give that bad boy a whirl and see if that helps your labor to progress. Again, the rocking motion and taking some pressure off your pelvis will help those hips to open up.

These are just a few simple suggestions of things you can do to keep labor going. I tried pretty much everything; what worked best for me was the birthing ball in the shower and then sitting on the toilet. That's one that I didn't mention in the list above, but with drinking all those fluids, I had to go and I ended up getting a ring around my tushy 'cause I stayed on there for so long. It just felt good to sit there. I can't really explain why, probably because it helps to open up the pelvis and relieves some of the pressure, all I know is, it worked.

I do want to mention that a common reason for interventions such as c-sections is "failure to progress." The fact that your labor is stalling or slowing down may mean that your body (and baby) need a rest from the contractions and the exhausting work of birth. I read about a woman who was in labor with her second child, her labor petered out, her midwives left and she rested for the next thirty-six hours until labor started again and baby was born two hours later. As long as baby and you are in good health, view this "failure" as an "opportunity" -to rest and be ready for the big finish.

takeaways

- Changing positions is crucial to keeping labor going if it's stalling out.

- Be a member of the 'hydration nation' and drink water, mama!

- To keep labor moving: use the rocking chair, climb stairs, do squats, or the birthing ball.

- If you and baby are in good health, take the opportunity to rest if labor grinds to a halt; get some sleep so you're ready to push.

nine

Stick a Fork in Me, I'm DONE!

Life is always a rich and steady time when you are waiting for something to happen or to hatch.
~ E.B. White

It's amazing how fast time flies the first half or three-quarters of your pregnancy. Then, for some god-awful reason, time stands still. So does your sleep cycle. Peeing, on the other hand, never stops and neither does the back pain or the cramps that make you sit straight up in your bed, from the deepest sleep.

You're all set, linens and clothes are washed and ready, car seat is installed and safety checked. You're ready to get this show on the road. You're all excited, then your due date comes and goes and nothing is happening. It's the most anti-climactic date on the face of the earth. For nearly 10 months you've looked forward to "the big day" and have thought that magically, a baby would pop out FOR SURE by this date. Why would the medical world be so cruel as to give you this date and then nothing happens? While some doctors will cater to your every pregnant whim and induce you any day after your due date, others will allow your body to go into labor naturally for up to two weeks after that magical (or not) date. Refer back to chapter two in case you're scratching your head, wondering how you and your doctor don't see eye to eye on this topic. We won't even say, "We told you so."

There is still some mystery and intrigue surrounding how labor truly gets going. Recently, researchers have found that babies release a substance from their lungs, signaling that their lungs are fully developed and they are ready to head out which in turn tells mama to release hormones and hence, labor starts. Isn't that so neat that baby and mama are working together to get baby out? Team baby-mama is in full effect!

Carole Woods Nichols, a midwifery professor at Yale, came up with a way to calculate your due date which takes into account your cycle length and if it's the first time you've given birth. This method is very different than the more regularly used "Naegele's Rule", which is solely based on 40 weeks gestation.

Woods Method: How to Calculate Your Due Date (First-Time Moms)

1. What is the first day of your last menstrual period?

2. Take that date and add 12 months. For example, we'll say the first day of your last menstrual period was February 18, 2011. Adding a year would make it February 18, 2012.

3. Subtract two months and 14 days. This would now make your due date December 4, 2011. If you have a typical 28-day cycle you are done and this is your estimated due date. If you have a longer or shorter cycle than 28 days, follow the steps below to continue calculating.

4. If your cycle is longer than 28 days, then add those days to your due date. Let's say your cycle is 33 days. Do some subtraction 33 - 28 = 5. Now add five days to December 4, which would make your estimated due date December 9, 2011. Thank God you paid attention in math class.

5. If your cycle is shorter than 28 days then you just subtract those days from your due date. Let's say your cycle is 24 days. Do a little number crunching: 28 - 24 = 4. Now just subtract four days from December 4, which would make your estimated due date November 30, 2011. Phew.

For second-time moms (or more):

Do the same steps 1 and 2 as for the other calculation.

3. Subtract two months and **18 days**. Which if we are using the same dates as an example and you have a regular 28-day cycle then your estimated due date is November 30, 2011.

4. Adjust for longer cycle length the same way as the first example. However many days above 28 that your cycle is, add to estimated due date. So if your cycle is 33 days. You add 5 days to November 30th which makes your new due date December 5th.

5. To adjust for shorter cycle length, just subtract the number of days under 28 that your cycle runs from your estimated due date. So if you have a 24-day cycle, then subtract 4 days from November 30th which means your new estimated due date is November 26th. Happy Thanksgiving! Now just bust out a baby and the cornucopia and call it done.

Regardless of calculations and equations, babies don't really care about our number crunching and planning, which make it impossible to predict exactly when baby will be ready to come.

Stay open-handed about baby's arrival:

1. **Use the Woods Method to calculate your due date.** Taking your cycle, and if you've ever had a baby into account is much more accurate than a 40 week rule. Each woman and baby is different!

2. **Count on baby coming later than your due date.** I found this very helpful. I didn't think for one second that baby would come before or on our due date (and was pleasantly surprised when he came 3 weeks "early.")

3. **When people ask, tell them the month or an approximate, don't tell them a date.** As well-meaning as people are, it can be frustrating when you're constantly asked when you're due, especially towards the end. This is a good way not to psyche yourself out.

4. **Don't take off work the week of your due date!** So many women and men use up their paid time off in anticipation that baby will arrive on the date specified. While it's important to be prepared, wait to take off work until labor is in full swing and baby coming is a sure thing! Twiddling your thumbs at home during "due date week" will drive you all nuts.

At the end of this journey called pregnancy, it's very normal to "be done." That's part of the way that God designed this whole process. He knew that in order for us to reach within and get the gumption to get that baby out, we'd need to be highly motivated. And we are. It used to be cute to have this little person invading your body, but the cuteness factor dies at about 40 weeks and every waking hour is consumed with getting this little person out of your bodily cavity and safely into the world.

Since 95% of pregnant women don't deliver on their due date, you might be wondering what happens now? This is a pretty slippery slope for healthcare professionals. There are many who have succumbed to the notion that scheduling an induction due to convenience is perfectly okay. Even the most birth-friendly midwives and doctors get really uncomfortable if a baby hasn't come by 42 weeks and will usually insist on using techniques to hurry the baby up and get things going before baby is really ready. Medical professionals assert that the quality of the placenta deteriorates after 42 weeks of pregnancy, but honestly, there is no conclusive research to support that theory. When you think about it, why would there be? Since each woman and baby is a unique individual and develops and grows differently, applying a rule that at 42 weeks, your placenta will go to pot, just doesn't make any sense.

In plain language, induction is ignoring the baby's time table and making things happen when we want them to for convenience, planning, or being uncomfortable reasons.

Truly, the only reasons why labor should be induced are if the safety of the baby outside the womb is greater than inside the womb. These reasons could include:

1. Preeclampsia (you have high blood pressure and protein in the urine.)

2. Water has broken and labor hasn't started within (about) 24 hours- there's a danger for the baby to get an infection, since the amniotic sac is no longer there to protect the baby.

3. You have a uterine infection.

4. Baby isn't growing.

I know of a woman who had her baby at 43 weeks and 5 days. This was consistent with the births of her other children, yet she was unable to find a doctor or midwife who would deliver the baby "this late" due to malpractice insurance stipulations. The woman birthed that baby at home with her husband, by themselves. Now, I am not advocating that every woman birth their baby without trained professionals around. I AM saying that it's important for baby to start labor, not our doctors, and not ourselves unless absolutely medically necessary and as an absolute last resort. Besides hurrying baby before baby is ready, the chance of more and more medical interventions becomes likely, creating a snowball effect, potentially harming baby, mama (or both).

For example, the mother is induced with Pitocin - this stresses the baby out- because the uterus is squeezing baby tighter and stronger than normal. The doctors detect that baby is in distress and need to remove baby immediately, hence a c-section.

Did you know that one in three pregnancies results in a c-section? This is twice the number recommended by the World Health Organization.

The United States actually has the highest infant and maternal mortality rate of any industrialized nation. This is shocking for a country such as ours and one of the reasons for this leads back to "intervention" or not allowing nature to take its course. Women's bodies and the babies that reside in them know exactly how and when to start, continue and finish labor. So while the term "induction" may sound like something reserved for rock stars and super star athletes, let me assure you that doing things on your time and not when baby is ready, can come with a price.

If the induction topic is brought up by your doctor or midwife, have an honest and open chat with them, ask lots of questions, evaluate the risks and the outcomes and then make your decision. This is why I can't stress enough the importance of the partnership between you and your doctor or midwife. Trusting your body, your instincts and your healthcare provider is crucial to making good decisions that are beneficial for you and for baby.

Being educated about birth options and choices you will have to make means that you need to know how some women attempt to induce labor at home and what some healthcare peeps do to induce labor as well. So here we go.

Inducing Labor at Home

1. **Sex**. I know. Doesn't it sound obscene? The very thing that got you into this hot mess, is the very first thing mentioned to get labor going? It's the kind of irony that should have ended up in that Alanis Morrisette tune aptly named Ironic (and had she been a mom at the time of writing, surely would have.) But it's true. Sex will get a party started, but maybe not the one that you want. The spermies have something in them called prostaglandins, which is a hormone that ripens the stage for labor. So a little "wham, bam, thank you ma'am" can prepare your cervix for labor but may not do much else.

2. **Castor oil or Enemas**. I hesitate to put this under the "natural ways to go about this" portion of the chapter. Mainly because since when is using castor oil or giving yourself an enema at 40 plus weeks pregnant considered "natural"? But since we're here, we'll jump in. Experts actually disagree as to whether or not this is effective in inducing labor, or if it's just another thing to make you miserable. (Same with eating super spicy foods to bring on labor.) The idea is this: give yourself diarrhea. Make your colon all spastic and freaky, which will then make your uterus think, oh my gosh, I think I need to get spastic and freaky, too. And so your contractions begin. Now, if your cervix is ripe for labor (and you thought ripe was only for bananas), which is also known as effaced or softened, then the chances of this working are a bit higher. Otherwise you will join the ranks of thousands of women who will have one more thing to add to their list of "expert tips that didn't do a stinking thing for me."

3. **Herbs**. There are lots of homeopathic-type, herbal things you can do, but you really need to know what you're doing. Definitely consult your doctor or midwife before you try any

of these concoctions. Primrose oil is one of them that can be taken orally or vaginally. Primrose oil contains that magic hormone (just like those little spermies) called prostaglandin. Your cervix may soften, which will allow baby to come down further into the birthing canal, which will eventually set the labor wheels into motion. Again, consult with your doctor or midwife.

4. **Walk 'n' Roll.** One of my friends was so desperate to give birth that she walked 10 miles a day for a week before her baby was born. 10 miles! I barely drive 10 miles a day, much less walk! While exercise is super good for you and for baby, walking alone will not be enough to start the labor train. Now, if it's a choice between walking and say, sitting on the couch eating potato chips, I'm going to go with the walking. But suddenly inserting miles and miles of walking into your day will not make contractions suddenly appear. In fact, if you haven't been exercising regularly, it's not a good idea to throw in some serious mileage. You definitely don't want your muscles to be sore when you DO go into labor and you want to have the energy and stamina for the big

event (and not use it up doing miles around your neighborhood).

5. **TITilation.**. When the ol' nips get some stimulation, they cause the release of oxytocin into the bloodstream which then tells the muscles of the uterus to start kickin' into gear with contractions.

My friend Kelli Stapleton, founder of BirthStoriesonDemand.com swears by this -stimulate the nipples trick- to getting labor going. In fact, she found two vibrating sex toys and repurposed them. She simply put these two little numbers into her nursing bras and let them titillate the girls for an hour each day. Guess what? It worked! Labor started after a few days and Kelli was one happy –and dare I say "ingenius" camper.

Whether it's oral, manual, sex toy, breast pump, or any other gadget or whoseywhatsis you can think of, the way in which you go about stimulating doesn't really matter- just get those nipples stimulated.

Ways Doctors/Midwives Can Induce

1. **Breaking the waters**— Your doctor or midwife may suggest breaking your waters to get labor started. This is done by inserting what looks like a crochet hook up your hoohaa and breaking your water. Remember when discussing this option with your doctor or midwife, that once your water breaks, you have a time limit to have the baby. This is mostly due to the fact that the sack with the amniotic fluid (your waters) is in place to protect your baby and once it is gone, the baby needs to come out fairly soon to avoid complications.

2. **Stripping Membranes**—This is when your doctor or midwife takes their finger (again up your hoohaa) and separates the amniotic sack from the lower part of your uterus. This usually releases those prostaglandins hormones which could get labor going.

3. **Pitocin**—A common form of inducing labor is the use of a synthetic oxytocin called Pitocin. Oxytocin is also called "The Love Hormone." Ya know after sex how you feel all tingly and usually have that post-coital glow? Well, it's all because of the Love Hormone. The very thing that got you here in the first place is also found in labor (contractions) and breast feeding (it causes the milk to be released).

Oxytocin creates this warm, nurturing feeling. It's the hormone that's responsible for mamas doing this crazy thing called birth over and over again. While we all remember the details of the experience and a bit of the pain, the oxytocin allows our warm and fuzzy feelings about the birth to overcome the pain aspect and hence we get ourselves knocked up again and again. The thing to know about Pitocin is that the use of it will bring about contractions that are a lot stronger than those brought on by its naturally occurring counter-part, oxytocin. Sometimes the contractions can be so intense that not only is it a lot more painful for you, it also may adversely affect the baby by creating contractions that are too intense for the baby to tolerate.

4. **Ripening the Cervix**— (You're thinking bananas again, aren't you?) Another potential option for inducing labor is for your care provider to insert a suppository (you know where) that contains that miracle hormone, prostaglandin. This softens the cervix and could get things moving so labor can start.

When talking to friends and co-workers who have used any or all of the methods mentioned, you'll hear lots of differing experiences about what worked and what didn't. The important thing to remember as 40, 41, and 42 weeks of pregnancy looms: in the history of the world, there has never been a person who has stayed pregnant for their entire life. This baby WILL COME OUT! You won't be that freak of nature who stays pregnant for five more years. Remember that and stay positive!

takeaways

- Use the Woods Method to calculate your due date.

- The longer the baby "cooks" in that oven, the better. Letting baby decide when he or she is ready to be born is best

- Remember that your due date isn't a "sell by date" or a guarantee of when baby will be ready, anticipate that baby will arrive a couple weeks after your due date, it will be a lot easier to stay positive that way.

- Your healthcare provider can do a few things to induce labor, discussing these options and how this all occurs BEFOREHAND is a good idea.

ten

The C-Section Scene

Stay committed to your decisions;
but stay flexible in your approach.
~Tony Robbins

When I was pregnant, I was pretty naïve as to what happens during a c-section. I knew that it was major surgery, but that's about the extent of it. With c-section rates hovering at about 30% (as of 2008), it is crucial, now more than ever, to educate ourselves about this event so that we can anticipate, plan and make informed decisions about our health and that of our baby.

A friend of mine, Heather, is a whole foods, healthy living expert. She is passionate about eating healthy meals, drinking loads of water, and making good, healthy choices in life. Heather was pregnant with her first baby and hired a certified nurse midwife to deliver her baby at her home. She was incredibly excited and prepared for this home birth. Heather's husband made the house cozy and comfortable, adding just the right touches of ambiance here and there so that their nest would be the most soothing, wonderful place for them to welcome their new baby.

In the days leading up to their baby's birth, Heather lost her baby cork, her water broke and she started experiencing really intense contractions. Heather's midwife arrived and assessed her and determined that she was only about 3 cm dilated (this was after 12 hours of active labor). Heather felt discouraged, but did her best to keep working through each and every one. The midwife assessed her a few hours later and determined that the baby was posterior (when the back of baby's head is against mama's spine) which is why Heather was having massive amounts of back pain (back labor). The midwife also told her that the baby's head was turned sideways. After lots of crouching and squatting and trying to get that baby flipped around and her head in the proper position, Heather was losing steam. She had not slept in 3 nights and had been laboring intensely for almost a full day. Progress was slow and because her water broke, there is a time limit—usually 24 hours, and she was approaching it quickly. They made the collective decision that it was time for the hospital. At this point, Heather wanted the baby out and did not want to feel any pain! Epidural was the first word out of her mouth when she got to the hospital. The doctor and Heather decided that a c-section was the best route to go due to a lot of other health and baby factors. And so Heather's baby was born.

In sharing this story with me, Heather said that she did not foresee her baby's birth going in that direction, but was so ready to be "done" that she gladly accepted the c-section (and drugs that go with that) in lieu of her home birth that she had prepared for.

Despite your best effort, plans or goals, sometimes a cesarean section is necessary. There are a few pretty common reasons to have a cesarean, these may include:

- Labor is not progressing (taking longer than expected) or the pushing stage is taking longer than expected. This is the most common reason according to Pregnancy, Childbirth and Newborn: the Complete Guide.

- The baby's heart rate is a concern (this is also known as fetal distress.) This is the second most common reason for a c-section and may be a result of interventions.

- The mama had a previous cesarean (though vaginal birth after cesarean –VBAC- is possible).

- The mama's health is a concern.

- The baby's health is a concern.

- The baby is breech or in another position. (Many hospitals and doctors don't like vaginal breech births, but they are completely possible. This is a perfect example of collaborating with your doctor so that you make the best decision for you and your baby.)

Here's what generally happens during a c-section:

First, you'll have to sign a consent form acknowledging that you understand and are okay with the reasons for the cesarean along with its risks and benefits. Next, the nurses will shave your pubes and then you'll receive anesthetic; this is usually a spinal or an epidural. You will not feel anything below the waist, but you'll still be awake. If it's a super emergency c-section or you're in a hospital with limited access to anesthesia, you may be given general anesthesia, which means you'll be unconscious for surgery. You'll also receive a catheter which will drain your pee.

Those mental toughness exercises, particularly the breathing and visualization, will really come in handy during this surgery. Stay focused and breathe. It's normal to feel nervous or anxious about what is happening, particularly if you weren't expecting it. Let the anesthesiologist know if you're feeling any discomfort.

The surgeon will make an incision, usually called a "bikini cut," since it's horizontal and below your bikini line (isn't that thoughtful of them?) If it's an emergency c-section, it may be a vertical incision because it allows the doctors to get the baby out faster. The doc will suction out the amniotic fluid and then will deliver the babe! The baby's head is delivered first so that the nurses can clean out the mouth and nose, allowing your baby to breathe, and then the baby is lifted out and wrapped up so you can meet him or her. Mary Beth Knight, author of Strategies for the C-Section Mom: a Complete Fitness Nutrition and Lifestyle Guide states that it is customary that mamas only get to see their babies and don't get to hold them until recovery:

> "Ask your partner to make sure to bring your baby close to your face, close enough for you to hear the baby's heart and feel the baby's breath, and close enough for the

baby to feel, hear, and see you. Rub your baby's little fingers on your face and your fingers on the baby. You won't have long; the nurses will want to get all the measurements and begin the Apgar tests."

There is a new movement in Australia and other parts of the globe to have family centered c-sections, where the mama can hold and actually start breastfeeding her baby right away while the doctor finishes the surgery. Measurements and other tests either wait until that first hour of crucial bonding time is over, or they do it while the mama is holding the baby, as long as the health of the mama and baby permit. This is something to talk to your doctor about.

While you're in LaLa land—after meeting your baby—your doctor will be working on delivering the placenta. I know. You not only deliver a baby, but you deliver a placenta. The placenta kind of looks like a slab of meat. I literally became a vegetarian after I saw my placenta and I'm sorry I have to use that visual, but you need to know what it looks like and you need to know that it's big and it's what delivered nutrients, took away the poo and allowed for gas to be exchanged for practically 10 months -kind of cool in a Discovery Channel kind of way. In case you were wondering, and I'm sure you were, the word "placenta" comes from the Latin word meaning "cake." I can't even make this stuff up. Once the doctor delivers the placenta, he or she will start repairing the uterus and closing up the incision. From start to finish it will take about an hour, writes Mary Beth Knight.

It's pretty normal during or after surgery to feel trembly and a bit nauseous. This could be from the anesthesia or from your uterus contracting. There are meds you can be given to ease these side effects but they may make you super sleepy so you miss out on really important bonding time with your baby. Instead, return to your breathing exercises or ask for a cool cloth on your forehead which may ease your nausea. If you still need some meds, ask for those that are non-drowsy.

After all this action, you'll probably be just a wee bit tired, anyway. This is a good time to bond with your baby on your chest, maybe take a little cat nap and try breastfeeding (if you're both able to do this). Mary Beth said that after her c-section, she really needed a bit of extra help to nurse her baby, and suggests that mamas ask for help. That's what the nurses are there for.

If you've never had surgery before, you may not know that a huge part of promoting healing after your procedure is to get you vertical and moving. Nurses will pester you at all hours of the night and day to get you up and roaming the halls. According to Mary Beth, the longer you lay around, the higher the chances are of developing blood clots, constipation and pneumonia. So when that nurse comes knocking on your door at 3am, remember she's there to free your bowels and help you heal. Movement also means blood flow increases, which brings oxygen and nutrients to the places in your body that need it most. So get movin', chica!

Recuperation

After a c-section, the general hospital stay is two to four days, according to Pregnancy, Childbirth and the Newborn: the Complete Guide. Use these days of extra help to plan out your recuperation time at home. See if your spouse, a family member or friend can help coordinate meals, errands and household duties since you won't be able to drive, lift anything heavier than your baby, vacuum, reach up to grab things from cabinets, etcetera, for a few weeks.

Allowing your body ample time to heal is crucial to a full recovery. Remember that c-sections are major surgery. Allow others to pitch in and help you during this time. Your body will thank you.

Because the number of cesarean births have increased 71% from 1996-2007- it is crucial, now more than ever, that you understand how potential interventions can increase the likelihood of a c-section. It is so, so important to talk to your doctor about what happens before, during and after a c-section, even if you're not planning on having one. Most people don't anticipate a c-section and are not prepared mentally or physically for the process or the recuperation. Remember back to chapter 5— the mental toughness chapter—a big part of our "training" is preparing for the unexpected and adjusting accordingly.

Since each doctor has their own methods and practices, it's important to know how they do things and why. Communicate to them your wishes and requests. If you feel uneasy about what they are telling you, get a second opinion! Yes! You can do that, smack dab in the middle of labor, at the hospital. You have a voice even when and especially when surgery is involved.

Many women I've spoken with have had a difficult time coming to terms with their emergency c-sections. Often times, the urgency, the fatigue and not feeling adequately equipped to face this possibility lead them to feeling disappointed, hurt, and suspicious of their doctor. One of my friends mentioned to me that she felt she had let her husband and baby down, that maybe she didn't do enough to prepare herself for birth.

While many c-sections are avoidable with a great doctor who is willing to listen to you and listen to what you know about your baby and your body, there are simply some c-sections which are necessary. But just because you've had one c-section, doesn't mean you can't have a vaginal birth after caesarean (vbac) for your next one, you'll just need to find a doctor or midwife –and hospital- who are willing.

If you don't glean anything else from this book, I hope you harvest the knowledge that investing the time and money to educate yourself about birth, your options, your rights, and what is the best decision for you and your baby will ultimately lead to a positive birth experience even if it's not the birth you hoped for.

takeaways

- Knowledge is power—Find out what happens during a c-section before your labor and delivery. Be prepared with the knowledge needed to make informed decisions, versus putting your trust blindly into someone else's hands.

- Make a c-section recuperation plan.

- Don't be afraid to ask for help after your surgery.

- Talk to your doctor; ask him/her questions about their methods and practices involving c-sections.

eleven

After Shocks - What the Hell Just Happened?

*If nature had arranged that husbands and wives should have
children alternatively, there would never be
more than three in a family.
~Lawrence Housman*

In the hospital, after J was born, I was unprepared for the toll that giving birth had on my body. I had spent so much time preparing my body for the arrival of our son, that I had not taken the time to really read up on what happens afterwards. I knew I'd be sore, sure, but I didn't think much beyond that.

The weight. I gained about 35 pounds during my pregnancy. This was a pretty good amount for my frame. Before I even left the hospital, I had lost 20 pounds. Boom. Done. I was shocked. I knew obviously that I would lose weight by the sheer event of birthing my son, but he weighed in at 6 pounds 4 ounces. I then birthed the placenta, another pound or so, and then all the fluid and so on. But 20 pounds? Wow. This was definitely an unexpected pick-me-up, but was, by no means an indication of how easy it would be to get the last 15 pounds off. So don't be fooled! Not everyone loses that much weight straight away, but you will lose a lot. Be excited. This is Mother Nature's gift to our postpartum self-esteem. It's a nice pick me up.

Cowboy. Our son was in the nursery for a few hours due to some respiratory issues after birth. As soon as I could, I got dressed and walked a very long walk down to the nursery to see him. I looked like I had been riding a horse for the better part of 10 years without a break. I seriously was walkin' like a cowboy, (no Wranglers, though). I felt a bit silly about this at first, until I looked around me and realized that I was definitely not a Lone Ranger and was in fabulous

company. I decided right then and there that I would embrace my inner cowboy, until I didn't
need to anymore, which was just fine by me. Giving yourself some latitude to heal and cope is so very important after you give birth.

Pelvic What? Standing in the kitchen talking to my mom the day after I got out of the hospital, I was completely gobsmacked when I realized that I was peeing on myself. I tried to stop peeing and couldn't. I actually started laughing and said, "Mom, I'm peeing in my panties right now and there's nothing I can do to stop it." I quickly realized that those kegels I had heard about were, in fact, no laughing matter. The pelvic floor that I had finally discovered had now collapsed and was nowhere to be found -I must've left it at the hospital. I faithfully did my kegels and elevator exercises from that day on and within a few days, my pelvic floor was back. Not to its old, strong and hardy self, but back nonetheless. And I sure was happy.

Until...four weeks later. My hubby and I decided to go on a brisk 3 mile walk at our favorite trail. I stopped to get a swig of water and hubby continued on, happily walking, pushing our Little One in the stroller. I decided that I had better catch up, so I broke into a slow jog. I was an accident waiting to happen and guess what? I happened. Quickly I realized what was going on and slowed to a walk immediately so as not to do any more damage to my britches than I had already done.

The moral to this story: DO YOUR KEGELS and elevator exercises! Write reminder notes and post them in your bathroom, on your computer, or on your car dashboard if you have to. I did. I drew a picture of a bagel (kinda rhymes with kegel) and left them everywhere.

It may take some time to recover your pelvic floor, but treat kegels like your BFF. Spend lots of time with them. They will show you their gratitude as you're jogging out to catch the mailman or sneezing or just plain ole belly laughing. It's been over a year and a half and I am seeing, now more than ever, the importance of kegeling. I'm even doing them as I write this. You should too.

To the Max. Part of the amazing weight loss I already talked about is due to a loss of fluids. I will not go into gross, painstaking detail—just thank the Lord above that the hospital so kindly provides maxi pads like you've never seen in your life. These things are so huge they are the size of a small country. My husband took it upon himself to take everything that wasn't nailed to the wall (literally) in our hospital room since we were paying for it anyway. That included these wonderful stretchy, mesh undies which are so super stretchy and comfortable and you can literally just throw them away when you're done, maxi pads and these FREAKING AMAZING circular pads dripping with Witch Hazel that was cold and felt marvelous on my hoohaa. We pretty much needed a small U-Haul with the loot that we left the hospital with. If you give birth in a hospital, definitely make sure to stock up. If you give birth at home or in a birthing center, ask your midwife to give you a list of supplies you'll need to have on hand. Places like Cascade HealthCare Products sell everything you need for birth at home. Just for fun though, you could have your husband go to the store and buy you some Depends, it's the least he can do, right?

Boobages. I have already delved into the fact that for the first time since I hit puberty, I bought a couple bigger sized bras during pregnancy. Besides giving birth to my son, that was the second biggest highlight of my pregnancy and I'm not ashamed to admit it. I purchased a few of those nursing tank tops from Target and packed them in my hospital bag. I wore those bad boys for a long time, especially at night because they provided some support (and I could put a nursing pad in there to soak up any leakage) and were also very comfortable. Be prepared mamas, 'cause after baby comes your boobies will be making colostrum, a very syrupy and concentrated type of milk which provides the baby with exactly what they need. Then your milk comes in and you'll have a boobsplosion. After you start nursing, your breasts will probably get sore, one of the best tits, er, tips I received was— after each feeding to use some of the breast milk and rub it around the areola and let it dry before putting the nursing bra back up. This definitely helped me to avoid cracked, dry, sore nips.

Varts. This one was a complete surprise. I was home, exercising, trying to get my "body back" and was doing a yoga pose. All of a sudden a gust of air went in and out my vajayjay and I varted. How could this be? It's been months? I thought to myself. I checked with my mom, a Pilates instructor, just to see if I was the only freak in the world who had a swoosh of air all up in my girlie parts and back out again, and she said, "No. You're not a freak. No one ever talks about it." So we are talking about it now, 'cause we just need to get it out there (so to speak). I was so self-conscious about this that I skipped my postnatal Baby and Me yoga classes that I signed up for. I couldn't bare the indignity of varting in front of people I didn't know, even if they were in my same boat.

According to Wikipedia-

"(flatus vaginalis in Latin) is an emission or expulsion of air from the vagina that may occur during or after sexual intercourse or (less often) during other sexual acts, stretching or exercise. The sound is somewhat comparable to flatulence from the anus but does not involve waste gases and thus often has no specific odor associated. Slang terms for vaginal flatulence include vart, queef [1][2] and fanny fart (mostly British).[3][4]"

I'm sorry. I got distracted by the Latin - "flatus vaginalis" and the British "fanny fart." Seriously. You can't make this stuff up. There's so much to say. I'll just say this- Do your KEGELS!!!

No Sleep. I was very concerned about the sleep deprivation involved in being a new mom. I've always been someone who isn't really a night or morning person, I'm a sleep person. Eight hours is just about perfect for me and I could be a professional power napper, I'm that good. I was pretty surprised with what happened after J was born. Immediately afterwards, that oxytocin was pulsing through my veins and I was literally through the moon excited and could not have slept if my life depended on it. I was exhilarated and on cloud nine. Then I crashed. I couldn't keep my eyes open but I couldn't stop staring at my new bundle of joy. We were so blessed with my mom coming out and staying with us for almost three weeks. Each morning after I fed J at about 6am, I woke my mom up and she would spend time with the babe. I would go back to sleep for a couple hours. This helped me so much. You may not have someone in your home who will allow you to do this, but everyone says it and it's completely true; "when the baby sleeps, try and sleep." The laundry, the dishes, the meals, those things will be waiting for you when you wake up. If you have friends or church people or a support group bringing you meals, even better. Or you can prepare meals ahead of time and freeze them. You'll be glad you did. You can also hire a postpartum doula to help you. Postpartum doulas provide amazing support to families after birth. They will do everything from helping with laundry, doing dishes, going to the grocery, to taking feedings during the night so you and your spouse can sleep. There's also a non-profit that is located in Grand Rapids that actually has volunteers who provide support (for free) to families after birth, it's called MomsBloom. Check and see if there's something like that in your area. If a postpartum doula isn't in the budget, this could be an amazing option. Or check and see if there are postpartum doulas who are needing to get their hours in order to be certified, they may be willing to give their services to you for a huge discount or even free.

On Call 24/7. I am not, by nature, a worrier. I've always been a "glass is half full" kind of girl. Then I became a mommy. Not that I started being a Debbie Downer, I just started seeing the danger in everything around me. I literally started worrying the second J was born. I was completely floored by this. Who was this worrying person? This question also coincided with my newfound status as being the IT person for my wee one. I was the source of food, clothing, shelter, warmth, cleanliness, nail trimming, bath giving, burping, spit up removing, itch scratching, everything. As control freakish as I was (and sort of still am…ask my hubs), I didn't really want my son's world to revolve around me. I didn't want the demands and the pressure of being his sun, moon and stars. I felt anxiety and the second we dropped my mom off at the airport to fly home, I panicked. I couldn't do this alone! And well, I wasn't really alone, but it sure felt that way. I took everything upon myself and did it all because I could and because I wanted my husband to be able to function so he could go to work and do what he needed to do. Moral of the story, I needed to get over myself and share the load. People offered to come over and give me a break, help with things and I gave them the "Nah, I got this." But really, I didn't. I needed help and that's okay. Strong suggestion…get over yourself and take advantage of any help that is offered. You'll be glad you did.

Postpartum Depression. It's very normal to feel the Baby Blues after you give birth. Feeling sad, anxious, irritable, crying, not being able to sleep, and having mood swings are all symptoms of the Baby Blues which can last days or even weeks.

Postpartum Depression (PPD) shares very similar symptoms as the Baby Blues, but the symptoms are often more severe, last longer and can interfere with your ability to care for your baby. You may also feel guilty, shameful or inadequate, and have difficulty bonding with your baby. You withdraw from your family and friends or you have thoughts of harming yourself or the baby. According to the Mayo Clinic, if untreated, PPD can last for a year or more. It is extremely important that you let your doctor know how you're feeling. Your doctor or nurse may even ask you at a check-up how you're doing. Spill the beans and know that you are NOT ALONE! One in eight women have postpartum depression, says Postpartum Support International, yet many women feel so guilty about their feelings that they don't tell anyone, which further isolates and deepens the pain. Licensed Professional Counselor, Melissa Meuzelaar suggests having a conversation about PPD with the people in your life who know you best, BEFORE you give birth. Educate them on the warning signs and symptoms so that after you've given birth, they can say "I know having a baby is life changing but this isn't you, this is extreme" which gets the ball rolling, in terms of getting support. Your friends and loved ones could be a great gauge to help you figure out if this is just adjusting or if this is something more serious.

As far as treatment goes, doctors will usually recommend talk-therapy or meds to alleviate this depression. You can also check out online support groups like the PPD Online Support Group.

P.M.S. (Perfect Mommy Syndrome) As much as some moms want you to believe they have it all figured out and do everything "right"…they don't. No one does. Take the pressure off yourself and allow yourself the grace and freedom to figure out the whole mommyhood thing as you go. People will offer you lots of advice and wisdom on how they did it. While this unsolicited advice can be helpful, you and your baby may be different. You simply have to navigate this journey on your own time and in your own way.

The mama that you see at the park that looks like she "has it all together" with her perfect outfit, her hair in place, everything packed all neatly in her stroller with her baby who is happily sucking on his thumb—yeah, she probably started out just like you. Frazzled, forgetting the all-important pacifier, diaper or extra change of clothes. She has most likely had public poopsplosions or projectile vomiting with no extra outfits to be found. Know this. Believe this. The reason that so many people offer you advice and tips is that they have been there themselves. I know I have.

Once when Little Man was a few months old, I went to a friend's house just to get out of the house for a bit. Before I left, I was running all over gathering things to take with me. I put J in his car seat and then forgot his pacifier, so I ran upstairs. I grabbed a blanket and tucked it around him since it was getting chilly out. Then I grabbed a diaper to take with me and we were out the door. I got to my friend's house, brought J inside the house (in his infant car seat), removed the blanket and was horrified. I had forgotten to buckle him in. We had traveled 10 minutes in the car; I had put him in and taken him out. I was horrified. I kept replaying all the "what if" scenarios in my head. I couldn't shake it. I felt so inept. My friend (God bless her) told me that she had done the very same thing. While I wouldn't wish that anyone make that mistake, I immediately felt better. I knew I wasn't a bad mom just because I forgot. And guess what? I never made that mistake again. But there are surely other ones to follow.

Mothers across the world make mistakes every day. This is an on-the-job-training sort of scenario. Every experience helps us to learn what we can do better next time. So get back to those breathing exercises again and relax. The next time you see "the perfect mommy" at the park, just know that she hasn't always been like that. There are many a ruined outfit, forgotten supplies and moments of sheer panic in her past. I promise.

You've got the Powa

During my own labor and delivery experience, I was unprepared for the power of intuition. That sounds all New Agey and obscure. But really, it's amazing how instincts really kick in from the second that we tune in and start believing in them.

After our son was born, he was having some trouble latching on-I had something called inverted nipples, which is as lovely and awesome as it sounds. Breastfeeding was difficult, but I wasn't about to give up. One morning at 7am (after the changing of the guard, er, um nurses) our new daytime nurse charged into the room, ripped of Jackson's beanie cap, commanded that I disrobe, shoved J's face into my bosom and declared, "He needs to eat. He hasn't eaten. He needs to eat." I welled up and tears started spilling over as she strode out of the room. I felt incompetent, I felt angry, I felt violated. How dare she march in here and tell me that my son needs to eat! The birthing warrior that I had been 24 hours before, turned into a Mama Warrior, "Oh no you didn't!" complete with neck moving back and forth and fingers snappin'. Thankfully we had attended a breast feeding class prior to labor and I knew that even if J had not eaten at all for a day that he was fine. He was born with a full tummy and while they assimilate to life outside the womb, they are built to withstand an adjustment period. This nurse basically told me that if he didn't drink my breast milk, they would put him on formula and I said, "No, you won't." I stood up for myself and my baby, my mama intuition was kickin' like a mule and I wasn't going to be bullied or pushed around by a, probably well-meaning, but bossy lady! I wanted her to talk to me woman to woman—to empathize and to find out the scoop about why Jackson wasn't latching and hadn't really eaten much. But she took one look at his numbers and shoved his face in my chest with the threat of formula and bottle feeding close behind.

So mamas. You have intuition. Tap into it, depend on it and trust it, trust your gut. You truly do have the powa—the powa to stand up for you and your baby and to really decipher what's important and urgent and what's not. Even though you're just getting to know your baby, you have spent more time with this baby than anyone else. If a doctor or nurse tells you something, check it against what you know to be true about yourself or your baby and then figure out the best solution. Doctors and nurses are educated and have a wealth of knowledge, but they don't know you or your baby like you do.

takeaways

- You'll need to reacquaint yourself with your body after baby. It's a new ball of wax.

- Listen to your momtuition. It's powerful stuff.

- Postpartum Depression is nothing to joke about; if you feel like the Baby Blues are lingering on and are hindering your ability to care for your baby talk to your doctor or find a support group!
You're not alone!

twelve

Breast Friends Forever

There are three reasons for breast-feeding: the milk is always at the right temperature; it comes in attractive containers; and the cat can't get it.
~Irena Chalmers

I probably should have laid off the National Geographic Channel while I was pregnant. There's nothing to lull you into a false sense of security like watching chimpanzees birth their babies and suckle them to their breast all while hanging one-armed off a branch and eating a banana—that's what I call true multi-tasking. I guess I thought that breastfeeding would be very much like that—except the banana and one-armed tree hanging part, oh and I'm not a chimp—I might be a chump sometimes—but that's a whole different ball of wax.

After our little bambino arrived, one of the first things we did was put him to my breast. Now, if you've been paying attention so far in this book, you'll know that my "rack" resembles that of an 11 year old girl. Suffice it to say that I was doubtful that my mammaries would be up for this big job of sustaining life for our little one. I was shocked when there was actually colostrum -thick syrupy precursor to milk that is chock full of vitamins and minerals for your newborn- coming out of my boobages! I was wild with delight, this equipment that I have ACTUALLY WORKS! I think I celebrated a bit too quickly though, as my National Geographic scene complete with baby at breast didn't last very long. Jackson had a hard time latching on and seemed too sleepy to even care. At this point in time, the postpartum hormones were raging like a Category 4 hurricane, I was sleep deprived and I was still in the hospital 3 days after Jackson's birth. I kind of felt like I had been in a casino in

Vegas for days and days; I had lost sense of all time and couldn't tell if it was day or night. Later, I realized that I had not even been OUTSIDE my hospital room for 2 complete days. I was a wreck and this breast feeding thing was tougher than I thought.

A ray of sunshine came in the form of my lactation consultant, who noticed that I had inverted nipples. What a startling revelation that was, accompanied by a (dun, dun, dun) NIPPLE SHIELD! Now this sounds like a companion to Wonder Woman or Lara Croft, but it's really the secret weapon of a tired and hormonally wrecked new mom. It's a silicone suction cup looking thingie that looks like it would be sported by Madonna as a fashion accessory— it is a super nipple with holes in the end. The idea is that baby now has something to latch on to while they're at the breast. It's genius and it helped me get through the first month of breastfeeding- until my nips were out and about all on their own.

Even after J figured out the breast feeding scene, there were toe curling moments where the pain of breast feeding made me want to crawl out of my skin. I later found out that I had mastitis, which is an infection of the breast tissue, and had some clogged ducts too. It was one thing after another, but I persevered and I'm so glad that I did. I had such sweet moments with J while he was nursing, staring at his face, seeing how he was growing before my eyes each and every day; I drank it all in, much the same as he did.

Breast is Best Because:

1. Breast milk contains thousands of different components that support the baby's immune system.
2. The baby will enjoy the perks of a supported immune system for the rest of their life. since the development of their immune system is impacted by breast milk.
3. Decreased likelihood to have allergies and tooth decay later.

4. Jaw, teeth and speech and facial development is greatly helped.
5. Reduced breast and ovarian cancer rates for mamas.
6. It's a time and money saver (and super convenient too).
7. You'll burn lots of calories breastfeeding.

Breastfeeding ~~Tits~~ Tips

1. Ask to see the lactation consultant at the hospital—even if it seems that the breastfeeding is going fine. They can offer helpful information and advice that could really be beneficial.
2. Make sure you stay hydrated while breastfeeding—a good habit is to drink a glass of water before you nurse.
3. If you have questions, there are valuable online resources and forums where you can pick up some great info like at kellymom.com or La Leche League.

4. Make sure to breathe and relax, this too shall pass. It really will.

You might feel like you have no idea what you're doing, but remember that **no one does** with their first or second or third or fourth…each baby is different and what works for one doesn't work for the other. Give yourself grace and keep trying different things until you find out what works for you and your baby.

YourBabyBooty.com had a Breastversation on Twitter some months back where mommies could ask Kelly Emery and Leah Tribus, both lactation consultants, questions. Here are some of the questions and responses.

After drinking one glass of wine or beer, do I need to pump and dump?

"You only need to dump if, when you pumped, you were drunk. One or two drinks right after nursing usually isn't a problem. Milk alc (alcohol) levels decline as blood alc levels decline. As you sober up, your milk does, too."

True or False: Mamas should wash their nipples before and after nursing to keep things clean.
"Those little bumps on the areola (Montgomery glands) secrete an antimicrobial to continually clean them for you!"

True or False: Pumping is a good way to tell how much milk I'm producing.
"The pump only gets 67% of the available milk. It's NOT a good indicator of what the baby can get. The right breast shield size can make all the difference in output. Those shields come in 5 sizes!"

Herbal teas…are there any that are safe for me to drink while breastfeeding?
"Most herbal teas are fine, but you can check out a book called Nursing Mother's Herbal for specifics. Anecdotally, too much peppermint tea can reduce your supply."

Any foods that will increase quality of supply?

"…Not unless mom is severely malnourished. Quantity? Try high protein snacks, oatmeal, fennel seed…Drink just enough water to make your urine pale; no need to over-hydrate. Over hydration can actually decrease supply. Drinking a glass when you sit down to nurse or pump is always a good idea."

I did drag my husband to a Breast Feeding Class before our Boo Bear was born and it was honestly the best class we took to prepare for baby, hands down. The breasts that we have are truly magnificent in every aspect. As I looked around the classroom, it was priceless to watch the men's faces as they learned about the miracle of the breast. There was lots of head nodding and wide eyed amazement; it was as if the guys were thinking, no wonder we love breasts so much!

For example, did you know that your body produces different types of milk, depending on the age of your baby? Your body knows just what baby needs as they grow and makes milk accordingly! Breast milk also contains water in it, so your baby is perfectly hydrated while they breastfeed. So amazing! Also, the size of your breasts has no bearing on how much milk you produce. You will find that the more your little one nurses, the more milk you make and vice versa.

Formula

Okay so breast is best, but what happens if that's not a viable option? Thankfully we do have the provision of formula which is readily available. The people who make formula try their best to mimic the amazing nutrition that your breast milk provides and they do a good job, but still, not all formulas are created equal. And as with everything in this baby space, you have some options.

You can buy formula in a powder (this is the least expensive option), you can buy liquid concentrate, you still have to add water (this is a little more costly) or you can buy straight up liquid formula, no need to add water (this is the priciest option).

There are also cow's milk based formulas, lactose-free options if your baby is having lactose intolerance, soy based formula, goat milk based formula and organic options. If breastfeeding turns out not to be an option and it looks like you'll need to do formula, have a chat with your doctor or midwife, research your options and availability and give it a try with baby. It may take trying a couple different types to find the one that baby will take and once you find it, stick with it.

I leave you with this fabulous mental picture. While I was pregnant (probably in my third trimester), I was at work and decided to grab some lunch at a deli nearby. I walked in and there was a mother breast feeding her twins, hands-free. They were sucking away, one at each teat, while she ate her sandwich. I couldn't stop staring because I wanted to figure out how she was managing to do this. The babies were probably 6 months old. Of course everyone else was staring (mostly the businessmen) because they were aghast that this person would do this in public without a covering. A couple months later, after my breastfeeding woes, I thought about this woman and wished that I had given her a big ole "high five" – though she seemed to have her hands and breasts full, so I don't think that would've worked too well.

This is just to say, do what works for you, mamas—but don't give up on breast feeding too quickly! Remember that your little one has been nestled in your womb for months and months and has been hooked up with all the goods via your umbilical cord. They need time to adjust to life outside the womb too and learning to suckle and breastfeed is part of the steep learning curve for you both.

takeaways

- Breastfeeding can be challenging and painful at times but it's sooo incredibly worth it.

- Use the lactation consultant no matter what! They have amazing information that you can benefit from.

- Don't give up. Go to the internet to find answers and connect with other women who are in the same boat. Breastfeeding is soo worth it, once you both get the hang of it.

thirteen

Getting Your Groove Back

*There is a secret in our culture,
and it's not that birth is painful.
It's that women are strong.
~ Laura Stavoe Harm*

It's been nearly a year of stretching, pulling, adjusting, cramping, eating, drinking water, tossing and turning—and that was before the baby came. Now that baby is here, it's a whole new ball of wax. Sleeping and eating cycles go non-stop. Changing diapers. Spit up. Poopsplosions. And the laundry. How can one ever prepare for the volume of laundry that one little human being produces?

Remember during this time of adjustment that you need to give yourself loads of grace. There will quite possibly be 500 items on your "must do" list and it's okay not to get them all done, like, right this second. In fact, it may take months. Thank you notes? They're very nice to send, but if you don't get them out until Junior is 8 months old, it's okay. Focus on the most important to dos, like taking care of yourself and your new baby. Eating and paying bills are good things to keep up with, too. And don't forget to drink lots of water—especially if you're nursing.

It was my birthday about 8 weeks after Boo Bear was born. Hubby treated me to an hour long massage at a spa 20 minutes away. I had some anxiety about leaving our son - mostly worried that my boobs would explode if I was gone longer than 2 hours. But I made myself go. I knew I needed some time away. And boy, was I right. Thankfully my male masseuse was a new daddy himself. He tended to my sore aching muscles with generosity and understanding. When I started crying, he didn't utter a word. He knew my hormones were raging and I was trying to cope with my life and my new identity as a mom.

The alone time in the car, coupled with that heavenly massage, did wonders for my soul and my back. I needed time to myself. I completely underestimated the way it would feel to be so needed all the time. It was both exhilarating and terrifying. And then, to hand over the reins to my very capable husband was also freeing and worrying. I tended to blame these feelings on my control freak-ish tendencies as well as my natural mothering instinct, which could pretty much kick Jackie Chan's ass. I wasn't used to being this "worrier," or as I like to call it, "warrior" mom. I wasn't comfortable in my new skin, my new role, my new job.

I came to find out that the first year of parenthood is filled with lots of these moments. Moments where the word "son" makes the hairs on the back of my neck rise to attention and my tear ducts get called into action. Moments where I watch my little guy sleeping and my heart hurts from loving him so much. Moments where I wonder how in the world I'll even be able to watch him grow up and go off to college and become a man. Why did I want this, again?

I made it a point to continue doing things that I loved doing before. For example, I got up each morning, showered and put make up on. I did this religiously, even if I had no plans to go anywhere that day. It made me feel productive and attractive and I just felt better when I was dressed for success. I also made time to blog (a huge outlet for me is writing) and to paint. I needed my creative outlets more than ever and really forced myself to do them, even if it meant not folding laundry or making phone calls. Reclaiming my identity as a woman, as a creator, as a writer, and as an artist was more important to me than folded laundry.

Owning My New Body

Besides adjusting to your new identity, there will come a time when you will need to adjust to your new body.

Thanks to this miracle belly cream that I applied religiously during pregnancy, I didn't have stretch marks. But I had lost my pelvic floor. My once wonderfully rotund and robust boobages that I gained during pregnancy and grew to love and flaunt, had shrunk into oblivion after I was finished nursing- to a size smaller than they were before I was pregnant. My once glowing and vibrant skin was having breakouts and I had melasma -dark blotchy spots on the skin caused by raging hormones. In a word, I felt completely unattractive and blah. I felt like a stranger in this new post-pregnant body.

As soon as my body would allow, I got to work and started exercising. I started with brisk walks. This was not only good for my body but also great for my mind. I made a point of getting out of the house every day. I gradually worked up to walking about 3 miles while pushing Little Man in his stroller. When I felt like I was making good progress, I purchased an at-home work out video. This actually didn't work so well for me. The workouts were about an hour long and I couldn't really get through a workout without having to hold or nurse my son. Winter was approaching, so I decided to join a gym. Little man was about 3 months old. The gym had child care and while I was reluctant to leave him there, I knew I needed my time. I started going to the gym about 2 to 3 times per week and it was great. Great to get outside the house and be around other people. Great to have a break from mommy duty —well, at least for a few minutes. While at the gym I did get called a few times to pick J up. He had been crying. I tried not to let that discourage me from going. Even if I got to exercise for 15 minutes, I figured it was worth it in the end. Every little bit counted.

{Two simple exercises}

1. **Transverse Abdominal Contraction** (I know, like you really want to see the word "contraction" again.)

This exercise will strengthen your innermost abdominals called the "transverse abdominis"—this is the very core of your abs.

Sit upright with your back supported by a chair or a wall.

Inhale deeply (your abdomen will expand). Slowly exhale (bring your belly button to your spine.) You can put your hand on your belly to ensure you're doing this correctly. Hold this contracted position for twenty seconds as you're STILL BREATHING.

Begin by doing three sets of these and gradually increase the number as you are able.

These exercises are really great to do when you're pregnant because the transverse abdominals will be the muscles to help you push the baby out.

Also, before you do any other abdominal exercise after pregnancy, check to see if your rectus abdominis muscles are separated-this is very common if you've had a c-section since the doctor has to actually separate the muscle to get to the uterus. Sometimes this happens as your abdomen grows and stretches while you're pregnant. The connective tissue between the muscles sometimes separates to prevent the muscles from over-stretching.

How to check for separation:

Lie on your back with your knees bent. Press the fingers of one hand into your navel (right above the belly button). Slowly raise your head and shoulders. The rectus abdominal muscles will tense and you will be able to detect a gap. A slight gap is considered to be 1 inch or less (that's a normal muscle separation). A 2 to 3 inch gap is a large gap and you will need to close this gap before doing conventional ab exercises (Note: the transverse abdominal contraction is safe to do and will help close this gap)

2. Pelvic Tilts

Pelvic tilts strengthen your ab muscles, will improve your posture and help to relieve back pain.

Lie on your back with knees bent and feet flat on the floor. Contract your abdominal muscles so that the small of your back is pressed to the floor (make sure you don't push with your feet or tighten your butt muscles while you do this). Place a hand under your low back so that you can feel your back flattening. Hold this contraction for 5 to 10 seconds. Contract your lower abdominals to tilt the front of your pelvis upward. Relax and then repeat.

There are several variations for these, kneeling and standing, and these are great to do when you're pregnant as well. For more information on these and other exercises, check out Pregnancy, Childbirth and the Newborn, the Complete Guide. Also Strategies for the C-Section Mom also has wonderful exercises for any new mom, whether you've had a c-section or not.

Currently I am about 24 months postpartum. I'm going to be completely honest and say that I'm still struggling to accept my new body. I know it's a process and I'm guessing that I'll probably reach that state of complete acceptance of my post baby body when I find out I'm pregnant with #2. It just always works out that way, doesn't it? And secretly I can't wait to be pregnant again…glowing skin and boobs! Heaven. (Oh and heartburn and peeing every five seconds…how soon I forget).

Sexercise

I don't know about you, but after our son was born, I was not a raging nymphomaniac. Sex had taken on a very new meaning for me and let's just say that it wasn't conducive to a healthy sexual life. Feeling tired, having our baby sleeping in our room for a few months and adjusting to my new post-baby body did not lead to being amorous. I was afraid of the pain of sex, my womanly bits had been through a lot and I was very hesitant to expose them to more jostling about. Honestly, it was very difficult for me to view myself as a sexual person. I was a lactating, breast baring, poopy diaper changing machine. Sex just wasn't important to me.

My husband (bless his soul) was extremely patient with me. We waited the requisite 6 weeks and then waited some more. My libido had taken a nose dive into the deep end of the pool and I wasn't sure if it would ever come back. Let's just say, that we eventually got to third base. There was lots of cuddling and hand-holding and some heavy petting. Once we finally did hit a home run, it was, well, different. There were no fireworks (at least for me). It was far from the suave, smooth sexplorations of our past. My boobs were leaky, the baby (who we put in his crib in another room) started crying, and I couldn't concentrate. It was hard (heehee). Things down South had changed. Hubby noticed it, too, of course but he was so encouraging and wonderful about it.

As far as advice goes, I've got nothing. Know that things will be different, but that may mean they'll be better than ever! Give yourself time and ask your spouse to give you some grace while you rediscover your inner sex-kitten. P.S. Dressing the part with some new lingerie could definitely help (wink wink nudge nudge).

takeaways

- Give yourself loads and loads of grace after baby comes. Skip the laundry and focus on your baby and yourself.
- Exercising is a great way to start reclaiming your body and your mind. It does wonders.
- Sexin' it up post baby is a whole new ballgame. Ask your spouse for some patience and some new lingerie.

fourteen

Putting it All Together

The moment a child is born, the mother is also born. She never existed before. The woman existed, but the mother, never. A mother is something absolutely new.
~Rajneesh

August 6, 2010, I woke up with a start and then relaxed in my cozy bed. I looked at the clock and smiled to myself. It was 7:30am and I thought I'd just rest my eyes for a couple extra minutes until I could hear Little Man rousing from his slumber. I imagined the day, one year earlier, when I gave birth to our little Boo Bear. I knew that J's birthday was not about me at all, but I felt a tinge of pride, if I could have hugged myself I would have. I did it. I kept this little guy alive for one whole year! Of course I wasn't alone, hubby was there with me. I survived sleep training woes, angst ridden date nights with my husband, recovering my pelvic floor, countless trips on airplanes by myself with a newborn. All the questions, doubts, worries and fears that plagued me for so long I had worked through, at least for that moment- another wave of them is imminent. I felt that same rush of empowerment I first had when I gave birth to J, the feeling that I could do anything I put my mind to.

As I watched the red bars on the monitor spring to life, I hopped out of bed and couldn't wait to wish our Little Man a happy first birthday. It felt good to be at this place. I had relinquished my life for a while to this needy little baby and was now reclaiming my new life and exploring the joys, triumphs and challenges of a toddler. I swear the next time I blink he'll be 18 and each time I think about it, my heart breaks a little. Being a mom is the hardest, most challenging, constantly amazing thing I have ever experienced.

Going to the MotherLand isn't for wimps. It takes strong, resilient, smart, hard-working, compassionate, selfless, giving (did I say amazing?) women to go on this journey of life giving.

Welcome to this amazing place mama. You can do it, in fact, you already are.

contact

If you have thoughts or questions about the book or any specific chapters or sections Sarah would love to hear from you as well. She reads and responds to each and every email.

Sarah is also available for speaking engagements, book readings or any other event, please email her for all of the above at: Sarah@yourbabybooty.com

Also, you can stay in the loop by following
Your Baby Booty on:

facebook.com/YourBabyBooty

twitter: @YourBabyBooty

about the author

Sarah's writing career started circa 1988. Armed with her Precious Moments journal, a pencil and an attitude, Sarah's entries consisted mostly of friend drama, boys she was chasing after, parental problems and Saddam Hussein-and the invasion of Iraq. Ya know, typical 10 year-old-girl stuff.

Flash forward 15 journals and 20 years later, Sarah was (and still is) married, knocked up and living thousands of miles from family. So she did what any person (who has a propensity to over-share) does, started a blog called **The Life of Blights** to keep her family abreast (pun intended) of all things baby. After Lil Man was born, a new door was opened and Sarah discovered her passion for birth and helping women prepare for it, so **YourBabyBooty.com** was born. Shortly after, she ditched her Precious Moments journals, upgraded to a laptop and started writing this book.

glossary of terms

Baby Cork- a synonym for the more grotesque and less popular "mucus plug"

Baby Tar- may be referred to as "meconium" -the initial type of poop produced by newborns, lasting a couple days.

Birth Sherpa- a term coined by my husband which is another word for Doula, birth support or someone showing you the way.

Boobages- also known as "breasts" "a rack" "bosom" or "the girls"

Boobsplosion- When a lactating mama's milk comes in and takes breast size to new, previously unreached, heights. This may also occur if more than 2 hours passes between feedings and mammary glands become rock solid and porn star-like before drenching your shirt at the first sign of your baby or someone else's.

Female Bits- these are the nether regions in your lower extremities, these include vagina, urethra.

HooHaa- another term for your vagina

Nether-regions (down South)- like we need another expression for vagina.

Poopsplosion- a phenomenon of Biblical proportions (at times) which usually involves one frantic parent who desperately tries to figure out how to contain the mess while also simultaneously cleaning it up. Bath tubs are frequently involved.

Spermies- a girly way of saying the very masculine, beating your chest type of word referred to by the rest of the globe as "sperm".

'tocks- short for the word "buttocks" or "booty" or "butt" or "bottom".

Thermom-an abbrev for the word "thermometer" which in this case, is used as an instrument of family expansion or containment.

Vadge- an abbreviation for the term vagina.

Vajayjay- yet another slang term for a woman's vagina. (This term may have been coined by Oprah.)

sources

Akil, Bakari. "*Psychology Today: Health, Help, Happiness + Find a Therapist.*" Psychology Today: Health, Help, Happiness + Find a Therapist. N.p., n.d. Web. 5 Feb. 2011. <http://www.psychologytoday.com>.

"American Congress of Obstetricians and Gynecologists." *American Congress of Obstetricians and Gynecologists.* N.p., n.d. Web. 6 Jan. 2011. <http://www.acog.org>.

Arendt, K., and S. Segal. "Why Epidurals Don't Always Work." *Obsteg Gynecol 2.*Spring (2008): 49-55. Print.

Belew, Cindy. "Herbs and the child-bearing woman: Guidelines for Midwives." *Journal of Nurse-Midwifery* 44.3 (1999): 231-252. Print.

Block, Jennifer. *Pushed: the painful truth about childbirth and modern maternity care.* Cambridge, Mass.: Da Capo Lifelong, 2007. Print.

"Childbirth Connection: helping women and families make decisions for pregnancy, childbirth, labor pain relief, the postpartum period, and other maternity care issues." *Childbirthconnection.org.* N.p., n.d. Web. 15 Feb. 2011. <http://www.childbirthconnection.org>.

England, Pam, and Rob Horowitz. *Birthing from Within: an extra-ordinary guide to childbirth preparation.* Albuquerque, N.M.: Partera Press, 1998. Print.

Garfield, Charles A., and Hal Zina Bennett. *Peak Performance: mental training techniques of the world's greatest athletes.* Los Angeles: J.P. Tarcher; 1984. Print.

Gaskin, Ina May. *Ina May's Guide to Childbirth.* New York: Bantam Books, 2003. Print.

Germain, Blandine. *The Female Pelvis: anatomy & exercises.* Seattle, WA: Eastland Press, 2003. Print.

Gonzales, Heidi. "How to Calculate a Due Date With the Woods Method or Nichols Rule" *eHow*.com. N.p., n.d. Web. 3 May 2011. <http://www.ehow.com/how_4917528_calculate-due-date-with-woods-method-nichols-rule.html>.

Hardin, Amanda M., and Ellen B. Buckner. "Characteristics of a Positive Birth Experience for Women Who Have Unmedicated Birth." *Perinat Educ* 4.13 (2004): 10-16. Print.

James, Kim. "EPIDURAL RISKS AND SIDE EFFECTS." Kim James, Certified Birth Doula - Home. *Kimjames.net* N.p., n.d. Web. 29 Apr. 2011. <http://www.kimjames.net/epidural_risks_and_side_effects.htm>.

Jeyasuria, Pancharatnam, Carole R. Mendelson, Julie M. Faust, and Jennifer C. Condon. "Surfactant protein secreted by the maturing mouse fetal lung acts as a hormone that signals the initiation of parturition." *Proceedings of the National Academy of Sciences* . N.p., n.d. Web. 7 Apr. 2011. <http://www.pnas.org/content/101/14/4978>.

Knight, Mary Beth. *Strategies for the C-section mom: a complete fitness, nutrition, and lifestyle guide*. Avon, Mass.: Adams Media, 2010. Print.

Kuehl, Karl, John Kuehl, and Casey Tefertiller. *Mental Toughness: a champion's state of mind.* Chicago: I.R. Dee, 2005. Print.

Labrecque , M, , E. Eason, S. Marcoux, F. Lemieux, JJ Pinault, and P. Feldman. "Randomized controlled trial of prevention of perineal trauma by perineal massage during pregnancy." *American Journal of Obstetrics and Gynecology* 180 (1999): 593-600. Print.

Levine, Carrie. "Maintaining your core and the health of your pelvic floor." *Women to Women "Changing women's health" naturally*. N.p., n.d. Web. 6 Apr. 2011. <http://www.womentowomen.com/urinaryincontinence/pelvicfloorhealth.aspx>.

Loehr, James E. *The New Toughness Training for Sports: mental, emotional, and physical conditioning from one of the world's premier sports psychologists.* New York, N.Y., U.S.A.: Dutton, 1994. Print.

Lothian, Judith, and Charlotte DeVries. *Official Lamaze Guide: giving birth with confidence.* [Rev. and expanded ed. New York: Meadowbrook Press; 2010. Print.

"Mayo Clinic." *Mayo Clinic*. N.p., n.d. Web. 27 Jan. 2011. <http://www.mayoclinic.com>.

Ochert, Ayala. "The Science of Mother's Milk." *NEW BEGINNINGS* Fall 2009: 28-29. Print.

"Promoting Pregnancy Wellness: *American Pregnancy Association*." Promoting Pregnancy Wellness : American Pregnancy Association. N.p., n.d. Web. 23 Jan. 2011. <http://americanpregnancy.org>.

Shaw, Gina. "WebMD - Better information. Better health." *WebMD - Better information. Better health*. N.p., n.d. Web. 1 Feb. 2011. <http://www.webmd.com>.

Shipman, MK, DR Boniface, ME Tefft, and F McCloghry. "Antenatal perineal massage and subsequent perineal outcomes: A randomized trial." *British Journal of Obstetrics and Gynecology* 104 (1997): 787-791. Print.

Simkin, Penny. *Pregnancy, Childbirth, and the Newborn: the complete guide*. 4th ed. Minnetonka, Minn.: Meadowbrook Press ;, 2010. Print.

"State of the World's Mothers 2011 Statistics and Facts-Save the Children." *Official Site-Save the Children*. N.p., n.d. Web. 3 May 2011. <http://www.savethechildren.org/site/c.8rKLIXMGIpI4E/b.6748295/k.BE47/State_of_the_Worlds_Mothers_2011_Statistics_and_Facts.htm>.

Stone, Joanne, and Keith Eddleman. *The Pregnancy Bible: your complete guide to pregnancy and early parenthood.* 2nd ed. Buffalo, N.Y.: Firefly Books, 2008. Print.

The Brain. Dir. Richard Vagg. Perf. unknown. A&E Home Video, 2008. DVD.

The Business of Being Born. Dir. Abby Epstein. Perf. Julia Barnett Tracy, Louann Brizendine, Michael Brodman. New Line Home Video, 2008. DVD.

"USA urged to confront shocking maternal mortality rate | Amnesty International." *Amnesty International | Working to Protect Human Rights.* N.p., n.d. Web. 3 May 2011. <http://www.amnesty.org/en/news-and-updates/usa-urged-confront-shocking-maternal-mortality-rate-2010-03-12>.

Weschler, Toni. *Taking Charge of Your Fertility: the definitive guide to natural birth control, pregnancy achievement, and reproductive health.* Rev. ed. New York, NY: Collins, 2006. Print.

Wiessinger, Diane , Diana West, and Teresa Pitman. *The Womanly Art of Breast Feeding.* 8th Edition ed. New York: Ballantine Books, 2010. Print.